BUY AND RENT
FORECLOSURES

---

3 Million Net Worth,

22,000 Net Per Month,

In 7 Years

YOU CAN TOO!

Joseph Neilson

Printed in the United States of America

This is not a work of fiction. It is based on real experiences, but names may have been changed.

Published May 2012

Table of Contents

Chapter 1: *How I Got Started*..1

Chapter 2: *My First Disaster* 4

Chapter 3: *Real Estate 101* 9

Chapter 4: *An MBA In 13 Pages* 14

Chapter 5: *The One Ratio to Die For* 27

Chapter 6: *1st Wonderful Niche: Good School District* 33

Chapter 7: *2nd Wonderful Niche:4/5 Bedroom Houses* 36

Chapter 8: *3rd Wonderful Niche: Section 8 Housing* 39

Chapter 9: *4th Wonderful Niche: Garages* 46

Chapter 10: *5th Wonderful Niche: Student Housing* 55

Chapter 11: *Making Ridiculous Offers* 63

Chapter 12: *How I Found the Houses*...70

Chapter 13: *Referrals: Assembling Your Team*..................................76

Chapter 14: *Contractors from Hell!* 79

Chapter 15: *Tenant Choice and Management*.....................................90

Chapter 16: *Smart Rental Rehabs* 101

Chapter 17: *Leverage And The Push Up Bra* 110

Chapter 18: *Legal But Soooo Naughty Nice* 118

Chapter 19: *How to Become Very Rich Very Slowly* 124

Chapter 20: *Full Disclosure* 130

Chapter 21: *Forms, Leases, Contracts, Specification of Material and Methods* 135

Chapter One

How I Got Started

It's January 1st 2005, New Year's resolution time. I'm 61 years old, no job, no pension, and Social Security, a fading promise, is 5 years away. I realize that whatever I work at next, it's probably my last shot at financial security. I sit down and write my new year's resolution in two words: Monthly Income.

I spend the rest of the day making up a mostly truthful resume, without a date of birth or high school graduation year and put it on monster.com. I brace myself for rejection or, even worse, zero replies. (After seven days, zero replies wins.)

Hey, what about franchises? I research the Web. Hundreds of them! Some are pyramid sales schemes. Most want big upfront bucks! And the products! I laugh at— Dog sweaters, capital needed— $115,000. Chimney sweep— $98,000. Three Dog Bakery— $268,500. The Egg and I— $275,000. Bras— $59,500. It went on and on. Nothing clicked. A wasteland of other people's dreams.

I'm really frustrated. Getting nowhere. I look down, my resolutions staring back: Monthly Income. I stand up, start pacing back and forth, a plan, I need a plan- a plan for me. What do I really want? DAMN IT! ME! I sit down and begin a selfish "I'm 61 and I deserve" declaration! To hell with what was possible! It flowed like a country stream after a hard rain. I rewrote it a few times to get it just right. Here it is.

INDEPENDENCE: I wanted to work my own hours— I would work hard and long hours at first— preferably without a boss directing me all the time. No suit, tie, or black shoes every day. But after five years (it's not like I'm 30) I wanted to work about ten, maybe fifteen hours a week. I needed time to pursue my pleasures – grandchildren, travel, visiting friends, writing, working out, watching sports, DOING EXACTLY WHAT I WANTED!

MONTHLY INCOME: How much? I called each number out loud, like an auctioneer.

$2,500 a month! My head nodded. Very helpful.
$5,000 a month! Yeah! Now that's real money!
$7,500 a month! Hell, what more could I ask for?
$10,000 a month! Something really magical about "$10,000 a month."

I sang it out a few times. So balanced, so simple. I swayed to "$10,000 a month" sung by Aretha Franklin. Hey Joe, tone it down... How are you going to get there?

THE OPTIONS:

- Corporate America: I didn't have 20+ years to climb the ladder to financial security, plus I wasn't a corporate type.

- Teaching: I had been a teacher for three years in the '70s, but substitute teaching wouldn't pay, was emotionally draining and I wouldn't enjoy it.

- Stock Market: The stock market was a crapshoot, another loser's game that I had not and would not win.

- Sales: I had been a good salesperson 25 years ago. But sales was a young person's game. You need energy, enthusiasm and resilience to shake off the constant rejection. A Willy Loman "Who's to pay?" failure was the last thing I wanted.

- Writing: I enjoyed writing and had self-published two books which didn't earn enough to cover the printing. Write a bestseller? Another crapshoot.

- Open a business: Had done that before. But selling what? To whom? Capital needed? Figured I could learn the basics in 12 months, refine it in 24 months, fully implement in 36 months and be well established in 60 months so that I just might have a shot at $10,000 a month. A long shot, yes, but it was the only path I could think of that might give me the independence and $10,000 a month.

It was 10 p.m. Emotionally spent, I went into the living room and clicked on the second half of a football game. A blowout. Remote in one hand, Budweiser in the other, I bounced through channels. ZAP! Young guy, happy happy, maybe 30, on a balcony in Hawaii, ocean waves, white beach and mountains in the background— beautiful. Said he was very rich, had a gleaming white very rich, very annoying smile, open collar, gold chains that almost covered his stand-up-and-salute chest hair. I laughed at the Bozo, but he kept mentioning money. Every other damn word. Then, like Jay Leno, he introduced a guest, a chubby, short female, maybe 35, single mother, three kids, had been on food stamps working two jobs at minimum wage— now had 17 rental houses, driving a Mercedes (picture came up). Single Mom couldn't be lying— pictures flashed of her houses.

Next, a thin, balding male high school history teacher, about 40. Okay, I thought, I can relate: off at 3:00 pm, summers and holidays to work real estate. Had been on Chest Hair's "System" for 18 months, had 7 houses with a goal of 50 and was aiming for $10,000 a month. $10,000 a month? I sat up, put the Budweiser down. If he could do it....?

Next a middle-aged Iowa couple, dressed for Sunday Church. Had bought Chest Hair's "System" three years ago, quit their jobs and were doing real estate full-time between traveling the world (YES!) and visiting their riverfront home (YES!).

$3,995! Chest Hair wanted $3,995! Dial an 800-number, give your credit card, fly to Florida (wasn't it Hawaii?) for a 3-day "Boot Camp" with Chest Hair himself. Come home loaded to the gills with a 254-page manual, a barrel full of CDs, and more forms, leases and checklists than Chest Hair had smiles.

It was 2005 and real estate was BOOMING with everyone-- everyone's friends, relatives, pot-bellied unemployed uncles, ex-homeless mothers-- all making millions. Seemed like every other channel had a real estate reality show like 'Flip This House' and 'This Old House.' It was difficult to pick up a newspaper or magazine without an article about folks making piles of money in real estate. Forget tulips! This was mania!

Maybe I was being foolish. But then again maybe this was it. I didn't have any other alternatives

Sooooo..........

Chapter Two

My First Disaster

Some Dogs Bark Beautifully on the 1st

"Open the door Joe," said the realtor behind me. My left hand pulled a rope handle attached to half a storm door, no top glass, one hinge; I held it open and knocked with my right hand. No answer. Knocked harder. No answer. Pounded. "Hello!" Nothing.

"Turn the handle and push," said the brave realtor. I did, and the ancient discolored wooden door, adorned with gashes and scars of battles past, creaked opened like an introduction to a horror movie. I entered cautiously into movie theater darkness, bed sheets covered the windows, my eyes started to adjust to outlines of boxes and stuffed garbage bags piled to about six feet. The no longer visible furniture helped form a faint ridge line from wall to wall. A small child with shoulder-length black hair, a winter coat on, his back to us, stared at a flickering black and white TV against the far wall. A large window to the right of the TV, opened into an alleyway, had no top half. It was winter and 21°. I traversed a windy path through the mess, past the stairs into a dining room, decorated similarly with boxes and bags, but also had half a ceiling, proudly displaying its wooden rafters. Next the kitchen, an add-on shack measuring 8' wide and 12' long, and needed total renovation. This Trinity (three-story small row house) was 12' wide but each side wall was six inches, giving living space of 11'. Like living in a miniature subway tunnel.

The stairs to the second floor were narrow and wound tightly in a half circle. No dressers or box springs could be brought up. Perhaps through a window, but that meant ladders and would tenants do that?

The bathroom had no door but did have a ragged 3' by 5' walk through opening into the next room, a large walk-in closet. The cast iron tub, brown with age, angled sideways on three legs as if asking for help before descending down into the dining room. The toilet, which rocked to the touch like a lead singer's hips, was opposite a doorless vanity, no mirror. Circular stairs to third floor. First bedroom on right was flashbulb bright pouring in from a 3' by 3' hole/skylight glaring down at two large orange storage bins, one half full of water, its twin completely filled. The next bedroom displayed a deco art gray mattress with cigarette burns playing connect the dots. How do people live like this?

"Not bad for $29,900," shouted the realtor, still on the 1st floor. I had seen 25 properties, made a few offers, was itching to buy something. This was cheap and cheap was good. The rehab? No problem. Get it done cheap. King of Cheap. I offered $23,000. They countered $26,000. I countered $25,000. They accepted. Four weeks, I was the proud owner. Figured $18,000 on the rehab. What was I thinking?

Painful MISTAKE #1
First Purchase should not be a major Rehab

Try to make your first few purchases a minor rehab. Something you can handle, based on your knowledge and experience. Be patient. Continue to look at houses and practice figuring the rehab's cost, to insure a positive monthly Net, using the Pre-Offer Property Worksheet[1]. Read, study and mark up the Specification for Methods and Materials, the invaluable Rehab Bible. Have an experienced investor or General Contractor, who also invests and owns rental property go through the house with you. They will make suggestions and hopefully alter the Exhibit A Scope of Work (part of the Independent Contractor Services Agreement) for the better. Keep working the Pre-Offer Property Worksheet till you know it cold. After a year or so you will almost be able to do it in your head. But still fill it out to make sure.

Painful MISTAKE #2
Choosing the Wrong General Contractor

---

[1] All my forms are listed in the last chapter

General contractors (GCs) eat soft-hearted, novice investors for breakfast. Read and study Chapter Eight, "Contractors from Hell!" I could direct 5 seasons of a general contractors TV soap opera—filled with lies, drugs, alcohol, rehab, death, hospital stays, arrests, jail, parole, divorce, murder, judges. I will stop. GCs cost me a lot of money and a lot of pain.

It is February, 2005, I do not know any general contractors, electricians, plumbers, etc. I ask for referrals from other Investors. I put an ad in the <u>Delaware County Times</u> and Craigslist and hold a General Contractor's Day at the property. I hand write a general description (my first attempt at a Scope of Work) of what I wanted done in what time frame. Fourteen GCs showed. Seven bid. Lowest bid got the job, labor only $3,500, me giving him money to buy materials, to be completed in 21 calendar days. I called the low-bid GC's two very good references but found later they were buddies from his last drug rehab vacation. Gave him a Home Depot credit card for materials. A week later nothing done. Then three months of great stories. (This is embarrassing, like going to Confession when I was 12 after my first date.) I learned I was a naïve, bleeding heart closet social worker, believer of sob stories, a giant excuse depository. The GC would work for two or three days (good trade skills, intelligent, persuasive as hell) then start his life and death melodramas, his need for money NOW!! He should have been a screenwriter. I give money, gone for three days, back at work with more Dickens-like stories, full of colorful, memorable characters staggering from calamity to calamity.

DEATH: his mother, then sister. **HOSPITAL STAYS**: him, his kids, relatives. **DIVORCE**: his wife filed, showed me the papers! **PAROLE OFFICER**: visited the job trying to track him down.

A visiting Municipal Inspector noted the GC's name on the permit and told me flat out he was a drug addict and would never finish the project. (It gets worse. I'm glad you already bought the book.) I wrote a "You're Fired" letter, handed it to him, told him what the Inspector said, gave him 10 minutes to clear out or I was dialing 911. Being on parole, that got his attention and he started packing. I stayed and watched what he took. Hired another GC. Total of seven months to finish the rehab. Final cost was $38,000 while I paid PITI[2] monthly (total $3,000), lack of rent ($4,000). Total rehab cost $45,000, 2 ½ times what I planned.

---

[2] PITI: <u>P</u>rincipal <u>I</u>nterest + <u>T</u>axes + <u>I</u>nsurance

The good news. Since it was in a good school district, town and block it rented right away and has stayed rented. But I advise you never to buy a 12' wide row or twin. My minimum today is 16' wide.

Real estate over time, is a forgiving mistress. Be persistent and your mistakes will make money. Today the property cash flows well, with a 30-year mortgage at 5.857%, principal and interest $257 mo, taxes at $145 mo, insurance at $36 mo for a total of $438.

RENT	-	PITI	GROSS = MARGIN	-	EXPENSES	=	MONTHLY NET	X 12	ANNUAL NET
1060/MO	-	438	= 622	-	180	=	442	x12	$5,304

Original rent was $925 per month. But with annual increases of 2.5% Compounding it's now $1060. Principal and Interest stay at $257. A beautiful thing. Owning rental houses you discover that on the 1st of the month some of your dogs bark beautifully.

Could you use $5,304 a year, probably tax free, in exchange for about 12 hours a year of management time? That's $442 an hour. Do I have your attention? Good. It gets better. Let's move on.

Chapter Three

Real Estate 101

"If you come to a fork in the road- take it"

Yogi Berra

I didn't know where to start. I needed a quick education, which would hopefully lead to a plan, what to buy, how to rent and manage to make money. So I went to the library (not much help), the Internet (almost too much), Amazon (cheap used real estate books), eBay (cheap used real estate courses) and researched it like a term paper.

I found William Nickerson's How I Turned $1000 into One Million in Real Estate in My Spare Time. I recommend you buy this out-of-print book on Amazon. Nickerson was the granddaddy of the real estate gurus and his book was a best seller in the early 1960's. He bought houses, fixed them up, rented them, then traded up to multi-family and later to apartment buildings. No hype. A dry read with outdated prices but excellent. Trudge through it. I believed I could do what Nickerson described.

Went back to Amazon and bought more used real estate books, sometimes for 99 cents. I joined the local chapter of several local real estate investor groups which met once a month and generally had a featured speaker and Q & A session. (I live and invest in a suburb outside of Philadelphia.) Before and after the meetings I mingle with investors, find successful ones and ask questions . . . lots of questions. The President and founder of Delco Property Investors (DPI) was particularly helpful and encouraging. She gave me her email, offered me her rental application and lease. I pestered her and others with email questions.

DPI is part of Pennsylvania Residential Owners Association (PROA) that held an annual conference, within an hour's drive, for three days with many national buy-my-course gurus speaking for one or two hours attempting to sell their manuals and CDs. I attended and again found other successful investors particularly helpful. If I liked a real estate course being offered I attempted to buy it used on eBay. I continued accumulating books from Amazon.

I liked the simplicity and abundance of residential real estate, as opposed to commercial, which seemed to be segmented into specific sub-markets which may take years to acquire the expertise necessary to succeed. Specifically, I thought rental houses was a simple business I could be successful at.

WHY I THOUGHT RENTAL HOUSES WAS A GOOD BUSINESS

The failure rate of small businesses is over 50% within five years. The failure (foreclosure) rate of residential house investors, even in these times, is considerably lower. And because of leverage (most of the purchase price is borrowed) you don't need hundreds of thousands of dollars as some businesses or franchises demand. Specifically, I learned that rental houses have a lower vacancy rate and longer length of tenant stay than 1 or 2 bedroom apartments, whose tenants may be transient with the average stay less than two years. A single person or couple without kids, has little holding them to the area and, tenant turnover is by far the single biggest expense. A rental house tenant is generally a family with kids, who connect to the block, neighborhood activities and hopefully a good school system. Think about it. Wouldn't it be much more difficult to uproot a family from their home as opposed to a single person or a childless couple in a 1 or 2 bedroom apartment?

I also liked that houses are plentiful. Thousands are bought and sold every month. And rental house financing is more common and available than financing a triplex, apartment complex, commercial building or a start-up business. A house carries with it an appraised value that the bank can loan against and foreclose on and sell if the loan goes bad. The bank knows it may have difficulty selling a triplex, apartment complex or commercial building.

I thought I could start with one house and if it goes well, then buy another and another. On the job training. If I lost money, made errors or disliked the business, I could sell the house and move on. So I decided to try rental houses.

The following is a list of questions whose answers gradually steered me into my current niche businesses. I recommend you read and write out an answer or guesstimate to the following questions. Your answers may change with future research and market experience, which is as it should be. Note: I did not have these questions and certainly not the answers when I started. But I wish I had, as it would have saved me time, money and pain.

1.   In what area, municipalities, or school districts should I buy?

I suggest within a maximum of one hours' driving time, preferably 30 minutes or less. Get on the web. Loads of information is available.

2. How many bedrooms (1, 2, 3, 4, 5 or 6) would be most profitable to own, given the supply and demand balance for each in your area? Who is my tenant in the niche with the most favorable imbalance?

    You may be, I was, surprised at the supply and demand imbalance for some niches. A high demand versus a limited supply means higher rents and, more importantly, LESS TURNOVER! Speak with other investors, survey the newspaper and Craigslist. Look for an imbalance in supply and demand. Research and make up a tenant profile. FIND A NICHE!

3. How much should I pay for the house?

    What are they selling for? Try any MLS website (Multiple Listing Services website, the one central listing place for all properties for sale), such as Realtor.com. Zillow.com gives you the present and historical value estimation of a house and also the present and historical valuation of the area. Very helpful. I use it all the time. Interview several real estate agents while seeking an experienced agent who invests herself or has Investor clients. Then go out and visit lots of houses.

4. Should I buy one that needs work or one that is ready to rent?

    All of mine needed work. I attempt to force $2 or more in appreciation for every $1 spent on the rehab, which hopefully will then be financed. Most foreclosures need work. Doing a rehab is not Rocket Science. See my Specification of Methods and Material in Chapter 21. Your first one or two should not be a house that's a disaster like mine, in Chapter Two.

5. How much rent will I be able to charge?

    Look in the local paper, Craigslist, and speak with other investors.

6. What Gross Margin (Rent minus PITI[3]) should be the Standard and Goal? **Standard** means which you won't go below (ours is $400 mo. or about 31%).

---

[3] Principal Interest + Taxes + Insurance

Goal is a number to shoot for, (ours is $500+ mo. or about 39%,) **Super Goal** ($600+ mo. or over 45% of rent).

7.   How much, on average, will it cost for maintenance, administration, vacancy and tenant turnover per property per month?

After trying different formulas I found 17% of monthly rent is about right and $8 a month for a garage. This estimate includes the budget buster Tenant Turnover. If your rents are much lower than mine, you may need 20% or more.

8.   What is the Standard and Goal for the Net profit per house per month?

Our **Standard Net** is $200 mo. **Goal** $300+ mo. **Super Goal** $400+ mo.

9.   How many properties would I need to obtain my goal of Net profit per month? Depends on your goal. You figure it out.

10.   What CASH ON CASH %[4] is my Standard and Goal?

Our **Standard** is 25%, **Goal** 50%, **Super Goal** 100%, **Grand Slam**: positive cash to you.

11.   What is my credit score?

Try AnnualCreditReport.com. The big three credit reporting agencies are Equifax, TransUnion and Experian. You are entitled by law to an annual free credit report but you must pay for the score, which I suggest you do. Start working on improving your score.

12.   What is my risk tolerance? Debt tolerance? Do you view debt as a bridge to success or a looming Grand Canyon 3000 foot drop?

My risk tolerance is high, but yours may not be. 'Know thyself,' said Socrates, who I am told, had twenty rental properties, which gave him the income and the time to wander the streets annoying people with questions.

13.   What capital (cash) do I have?

Cash is the numbers in the bank, stock market, IRA (can be invested in real estate, 401, or valuables, such as gold that can be turned into cash. What money can I borrow? From banks, private lenders and Hard Money Lenders. Then we have family, spouse and friends. Perhaps an Equity Line against your house, or

---

[4] Cash on Cash % is a very important tool that I further explain in Chapter 5.

refinance your house. And finally, how much cash can you pull from your credit cards?[5]

Your answers should change several times and go through many drafts, better preparing you for the marketplace, which will then alter them again. But that's good. You always must adjust to the marketplace you find at that time in your area.

Knowledge acts as a Jedi force field protecting you from making game-ending errors. You don't need extraordinary insight or intelligence to succeed. You do need to know what business or niche you are entering, then adopt simple rules and achievable standards.

Books I found helpful:

- Building Wealth One House at a Time by John Schaub   Excellent.
- Buy and Hold by David Schumacher, Ph.D.   Hold. A beautiful word.
- Down To Earth Landlording by Donald Beck   I use his lease, which I alter.
- Investing in Real Estate by Gary W. Eldred, Ph.D.   An Education.
- Landlording on Autopilot by Mike Butler   Funny, filled with information.
- The Landlord's Kit by Jeffrey Taylor,   Excellent on management.
- The Section Eight Bible by Michael McLean and Nick Cipriano, The inventors of The Eliminators!

---

[5] Chapter 17 further explains how to gain capital

Chapter Four

An MBA In 13 Pages

"To be a successful investor people don't need extraordinary insight or intelligence. What they need is the character to adapt simple rules and stick to them."

-- Benjamin Graham, *The Intelligent Investor*

The above quote is comforting since I don't have extraordinary insight or intelligence. However the adopting of simple rules is a core focus of this book. Within this context however, you must also avoid greediness and over-enthusiasm. That's a silly thing to say because I know people won't do it. It's not human nature.

The chapter title "An MBA in 13 Pages" is a supercilious boast that sets a rather high bar. But let's dive right into the generally accepted truths of investing and forming a good business.

Studies have shown there are four major rules for accumulating the capital to invest with.

1)   **CONTROL YOUR EXPENSES:** Spend less than you make, pay off credit cards, make up a budget, follow the budget, buy used, shop Walmart/Internet etc, be cheap.

"Annual income 20 pounds, annual expenditure 19.6, result happiness. Annual income 20 pounds, annual expenditure 20.6, result misery." - **Charles Dickens**

2)   **SAVE MORE:** Every month set aside a certain amount of money, put it into the bank, 401K, IRA. Pay yourself first. Think of saving as a bill that must be paid. If your employer has a 401K whereby they match your contributions, contribute the maximum out of your paycheck each period.

"Research has shown that managing savings and spending rates are the biggest budget determinant of financial success." - **Charles Schwab, *On Investing***

3)   **INVEST PRUDENTLY AND CONSISTENTLY:** Don't try to beat any market, indicator, goal or person. No need to reach for the gold ring. Slow and steady wins the race.

"Successful investing isn't about knowing more than anyone else. It's about having the discipline to stick with your plan regardless of the latest headlines." - **Austin Pryor, Sound Mind Investing**

4)   **MANAGE RISK:** All investments carry risk. Home run sluggers strike out a lot. Good investors are content to hit singles and an occasional home run. Investment mistakes are costly. If you experience a 25% decline in profit or equity, you must increase the current profit or equity by 50% just to break even. A 50% decline means a 100% increase to break even. Avoid things that seem too good to be true. Stay on solid ground. If you make an error, acknowledge and correct it quickly. Remember the get rich quick scams don't seem like scams at the time.

"Panic and greed are not investment strategies".-**Liz Saunders, *Charles Schwab & Co.***

*"I'm not so much concerned about the return on my money as the return of my money."***Will Rogers, 1933**

OK, so you are now saving money to invest in your own business! But what business? Will it be a good business?

THE FIVE QUESTIONS OF PETER DRUCKER

1) WHAT IS YOUR MISSION? WHAT BUSINESS ARE YOU IN?
2) WHO IS YOUR CUSTOMER?
3) WHAT DOES THE CUSTOMER VALUE?
4) WHAT ARE YOUR RESULTS?
5) WHAT IS YOUR PLAN?

The above are Peter Drucker's five basic business questions to answer as you form your business. The concepts apply to all businesses but we will focus on how they shaped my business plan, defined my numerical success and failure and how I was able to profit in the longest recession since the great depression.

Peter Drucker, consultant and author, is called the Father of Modern Business Management. When consulting with Fortune 500 CEOs, entrepreneurs or non-profits, he would ask the five questions. With insightful probes Drucker and client would uncover the actual business they were in, that is, what they were really selling, and to whom. It is not as easy as it sounds.

Cadillac - does it sell cars? Or status and success? Or the thrill of 400 horses? Or a combination? To whom? And to whom would they like to sell?

Proctor and Gamble - does it sell household consumables? Or leisure? Or cleanliness? Or time savers? To whom? (The all-American mom smiling at her 2 beautiful overachieving kids playing in the white picket fenced back yard?)

Apple - does it sell beautifully designed music players, phones and computers? Or group cool? Status? Simplicity? To whom?

Wal-Mart - does it sell medium quality goods to the lower and middle class? Or saving money? One stop shopping? All three?

Nieman Marcus - does it sell upper-crust quality goods or a feel-good I'm-important buying experience?

I suggest you read Peter Drucker's <u>The Five Most Important Questions You Will Ever Ask Your Organization.</u> If you uncover your own good business' answers, you have earned 50% of your MBA.

Write a Mission Statement for your business answering Drucker's questions. Have your wife, partner, others in the business or an advisor/consultant give input. It's not easy. A mission statement is NOT an up-in-the-sky, platitude-filled, aren't we all just wonderful. Has to be true, direct, doable and easily understood. The numbers and business plan must follow and make profitable sense. It must be a "good business" with a niche. Here's mine:

DELCO HOME RENTALS' MISSION STATEMENT

Delco Home Rentals provides rehabbed, spacious, low maintenance, four and five bedroom homes in safe neighborhoods and good school districts to well screened Home Visited Section 8 Tenants. We provide superior and timely service with a friendly but firm manner. Our goal is a 7% annual Tenant turnover and an average Tenant stay of five years. We plan to own 75 houses netting over $25,000 a month by 2015.

Garages: We acquire garages with the purchase of a house and perform a minor rehab. Our garages are safe, secure, dry, and used for (a) storage and work areas, sometimes with electric, in good neighborhoods for local vintage car/motorcycle enthusiasts and (b) work areas with electric for contractors. Our goal is an average Tenant stay of five years. We plan to have 25 garages by 2015.

Student Housing: We provide rehabbed, no party, well-appointed, low maintenance five and six bedroom houses, with adequate parking, within two miles of Concord University. We provide friendly but firm service with a goal of no vacancies.

Our **Gross Margin Standard** is $400 a month with a **Net Standard** of $200 a month.

WHAT BUSINESS ARE YOU IN? ARE YOU IN A GOOD OR BAD BUSINESS? DOES IT HAVE A WIDE, NARROW OR NO NICHE?

Warren Buffet, the Oracle of Omaha, is generally considered the greatest investor in modern times, invests in good businesses that he understands. He defines a good business as one surrounded by a wide moat protecting it against competitive encroachment of its pricing power and Net income. Some businesses, with an imbalance in supply and demand favoring their pricing power, can raise prices and increase their Net because they are protected from powerful price competition. Good businesses, for a variety of reasons, have a high barrier (moat) to enter their market. This moderates competition on price. A good small business does not sell a commodity by price cutting. The commodity business is a bad business unless you are the 800 pound gorilla i.e. Wal-Mart, Amazon, Target, Kohls, Home Depot etc. Bad businesses: think bars, restaurants, gas stations, hardware stores, small fitness centers, most small retail or internet stores or any small business competing against an 800 lb gorilla.

The following are examples of good business with wide moats:

COKE - They have created an unassailable marketing position in the mind of their customers. You don't order a soda, you order a Coke. Worldwide dominance. Non-stop marketing. High Gross Margin. Average return of investment (ROI) over 20% annually. Warren Buffet owns millions of shares.

BURLINGTON NORTHERN - Is a new competitor going to lay tracks across America? Rail is cheaper, uses less energy per ton moved, is more environmentally friendly than trucks, planes or ships. Warren owns millions of shares.

KINDER MORGAN MANAGEMENT, LLC - Owns the pipelines that send oil and natural gas throughout the United States. They are toll takers with very little competition. It would take billions to enter their business. Wonderful pricing power.

Only enter a good business with marginal competition; Compound your gross margin and net profit year after year. During a recession, or worse, you will stay in business while others die. In the rebound you are even stronger.

"When a manager with a good reputation meets a business with a bad reputation it is the business that retains its' reputation."- **Warren Buffett**

The following are Delco Home Rentals' good businesses and why they have moats protecting our pricing power and Net.

A) 4/5 BEDROOM HOUSES IN GOOD SCHOOL DISTRICTS TO WELL SCREENED HOME VISITED SECTION 8 TENANTS

In the five good school districts in which we operate, our houses are predominantly rows or twins, all of which are 65 years or older. 70% of the entire house inventory in our county has three bedrooms, 15% two bedrooms and 15% four or more. Any house with four or more bedrooms that is less than 50 years old, is a single detached and too expensive to buy, rent and make money. There are no moderately priced 4/5 bedroom apartments in our area. Therefore, supply cannot grow, and demand will continue to exceed the supply because there are many underperforming and unsafe school districts. Good school districts are in demand. However if the market changes, which is unlikely in the foreseeable future, I can always rent the four bedroom houses to three bedroom prospects, give them an extra bedroom, den and a powder room and still make money. Or start a Rent to Own program.

B) GARAGES: You cannot build a garage (or self storage space) and compete price per square foot with existing garages that have no purchase price, taxes, insurance, and very little maintenance. Demand for storage is strong as evidenced by the dramatic growth of the self-storage business. But we don't compete directly with self-storage as our garages are larger with electric available in some. We store cars, motorcycles, trucks, one plane, and give contractors a place to store and work.

C) STUDENT HOUSING: Concord University is growing. Four dormitories ($600-700+ per mo per bedroom including food and utilities) on campus without land to build others. Campus is located in a town that has predominantly single detached 3 bedroom housing. The town's two bedroom apartment complexes are converting some buildings for "students only" at $450 a bedroom including heat and electric. One cannot build a four, five or six bedroom house and rent to students and make money. DHR will continue to purchase old large houses in need of rehab and convert them to student housing. We will stay within two miles, preferably one mile, provide housing amenities, and charge between $300 and $350 a bedroom excluding utilities.

I am not indicating my niches are your niches. Each geographical area has its own supply and demand fulcrum. My three niches are applicable to my area, as I live in the suburbs of a large east coast city (Philadelphia) with plenty of older row and twin houses, some having a detached garage. I live two miles from Concord University. It is up to you to research the marketplace in your area and come up with your own niches. It's the first important step to profitability.

Pick up your local paper and spend time analyzing the different houses and apartments for rent. Go to local real estate investor meetings and ask investors what they are investing in and how they are doing? Can they re-rent easily when they have a vacancy? Do they have high Tenant Turnover? Get them aside at lunch where they feel free to talk. People don't want to advertise they are failing. Visit them at their place of business, walk through a few of their rentals. Do your homework. Date different rental bedroom types before you get married to one or more. When a good niche appears, you may ask yourself, "Is this real?" "Why isn't everyone fulfilling this market?"

Other niches real estate investors are in:
1. Students - Students or students with amenities, bed sheet changing.
2. Studios, one bedroom, two bedroom apartments - in areas lacking supply, with good demand, many times to narrow markets.
3. Seniors - Studio 1, 2 bedroom apartments for seniors or for working women (you cut the lawn, give other services.)
4. Hospital personnel - adjacent to the hospital, nurses, doctors, administrative.
5. Downtown metropolitan areas - young professionals, college educated.
6. Adjacent to Government.
7. Disabled - 1st floor, ramp; disabled, possibly with meals.
8. Adjacent to Industry.
9. Executive Rental, studio/one bedroom apartments for the weekday executives, i.e.: Washington DC by the Capital.
10. Military - Are you near a base? Good demand for 2 bedroom apartments.
11. Vacation Rentals - various websites set up for this, picture important, VRBO.com is the dominant site.
12. Bed and Breakfast.
13. Event Rentals.
14. Fraternity/Sorority/Club Student Houses.

Niches are limited only by your area and imagination. In speaking with other successful investors, I find they have a niche, generally don't call it such, but they specialize their offerings to a specific client base. When I speak with investors who are struggling financially, they invariably own a commodity, renting a two or three bedroom house to anyone who calls, perhaps in a bad school district. Too many houses or apartments chasing too few renters. Bad business.

A PRIMER OF REAL ESTATE BUSINESS TERMS

1) PURCHASE PRICE: The price of the House. In my area at this time (2011) with a flood of bank owned foreclosures (Real Estate Owned properties or REOs). I attempt to buy row or twin homes for $25,000 or detached homes for $40,000 or less. It may be different in your area. Log onto Realtor.com. Mix with and ask investors. Consult with real estate agents.

2) HUD 1: This is the settlement sheet that has all the costs assigned to the buyer and seller. You should receive one before settlement; if not, ask for one and study it. Ask questions. Banks, title companies, realtors (everyone) love to jump in with fees. Much easier to demand/negotiate before settlement than during. If I settle with mortgage financing it is even more important to get the fees before settlement. If I buy cash (ask the title company to hold the title insurance "open" for one year), then rehab, then settle with permanent financing, I expect the total settlement cost for both settlements to be less than $5,000.

3) PRINCIPAL AND INTEREST (P&I): The way you pay off the loan. An easy way to figure out the payment amount is with an interest/amortization calculator or book or use the following FACTORS PER THOUSAND. Take the factor (chart below that corresponds to your interest rate and number of years of the mortgage or amortization schedule) and times it against the principal of the mortgage.

Int. Rate	FACTOR 20 yr mortgage	FACTOR 30 yr mortgage
4.0%	6.06	4.77
4.5%	6.32	5.06
5.0%	6.60	5.37
5.5%	6.88	5.68
6.0%	7.17	6.0
6.5%	7.46	6.33
7.0%	7.76	6.66
7.5%	8.06	7.0
8.0%	8.37	7.34
8.5%	8.68	7.69
9.0%	9.0	8.05

	FACTOR	FACTOR
	20 yr mortgage	30 yr mortgage
Int. Rate		
9.5%	9.33	8.41
10.0%	9.66	8.78

Examples:

(A) House price $200,000, LTV[6] 80%, 5.0% interest rate, 30 yr mortgage.

$200,000

x 80% LTV

$160,000 x 5.37 (Mortgage factor) = $859.20 payment per month.

(B) House price $120,000, LTV 70%, 6% interest rate, 20 yr mortgage.

$120,000

x 70% LTV

$84,000 x 7.17 (Mortgage factor) = $602.28 payment per month.

4) PITI: P - Principal, I - Interest, T - Taxes, I - Insurance

PI – 70k 7.5%, 20yrs = $560 mo	
Taxes	+ $225 mo
Insurance	+ $40 mo
	$825 mo

5) TAXES AND INSURANCE: Taxes will usually include school tax, municipal tax and county tax. The county tax generally gives each house a 'fair market value' and an assessment, which is a percentage of the fair market value.

Tax Appeals: Because I am currently buying well below assessment, which is 64% of Fair Market Value, I HAVE STARTED APPEALING. I pay a modest fee ($325) for a full appraisal by an established appraiser. I have hired an attorney who takes 25% of the first year savings as payment to represent me. Kind of like a commissioned sales person. If the lawyer must sue, then his commission goes to 60% plus costs. The tax savings go directly to Net and cutting taxes feels wonderful. I am being successful in the appeals… try it!

Insurance - make sure your insurance agent works with real estate investors with over five properties. I have $1,000,000 of liability per property with a $4,000,000 umbrella on top. Fire insurance for 80% of $80 to $100 times (depending on the type of the house) the internal square feet with a $2,500 deductible. Insurance usually runs $40-$50 a month.

---

[6] LTV: Loan to Value. Percentage of loan to the Appraised value of the Property.

6) RENT: What the market will bear. We use a 2.5% annual rental adjustment. We believe in the power of Compounding.

7) GROSS MARGIN (GM): | Rent – PITI = Gross Margin |

GM is what you take expenses out of. Increases in GM have a dramatic effect on Net.

Annual rent increases, compounded, magnifies GM as the Net explodes as illustrated in the box below. Our current GM averages 40% of rent. We hope to increase that.

GROSS MARGIN AND NET MAGIC

RENT	-	PITI	=	GM	-	EXPENSES 17%	=	MO NET	x 12	ANNUAL NET
$1300	-	800	=	500 (38%)		221		279 (21%)	x 12	$3,348 (21%)
Rent Increase of 2.5% or $33										
1333	-	800	=	533 (40%)	-	226	=	307 (23%)	x 12	$3,684 (23%)
2.5%				**7% increase**				**10% increase**		**10% increase**
Rent Increase of 4% or $52										
1352	-	800	=	552 (41%)	-	230	=	322 (24%)	x 12	$3,864 (24%)
4%				**10% increase**				**15% increase**		**15% increase**
Rent Increase of 8% or $104										
1404	-	800	=	604 (43%)	-	239	=	365 (26%)	x 12	$4,380 (26%)
8%				**21% increase**				**31% increase**		**31% increase**

This is why you want a "Good Business" with a moat surrounding your power to increase rents. By increasing your rents, the GM takes off and the Net soars. The awesome power of Compounding! Our **Standard**, not to go below, is a GM of $400/mo or 31%. **Goal** $500/mo or 39%. **Super Goal!** $600/mo or about 45%.

8) NET | Gross Margin- Expenses = NET |

As illustrated above and in Chapter Twenty, How To Get Very Rich Very Slowly, a small (2.5%) annual rental increase over a ten year span, even with correspondingly small (2.5%) increase in Insurance (doubtful), Taxes (yes) and Expenses (try hard not to) we have a 70% Net increase after 10 years. As illustrated an 8% rent increase pushes the Net to 32%. Small, consistent compounded increases in rent flows to the GM and will exponentially increase the NET.

Correspondingly, a decrease in Expenses goes directly to Net. Yes, that's 100%. It's why ruthless corporate cost cutters are so successful and valuable. Every dollar saved goes to Net then x 12 for the year. Our **Standard Net** is $200 mo, **Goal** $300 mo, **Super Goal** $400 mo.

9) EXPENSES: In our initial rehab, we attempt to make the house Maintenance Request proof. We do EVERYTHING to eliminate future maintenance. This is covered in Chapter 14, "Contractors from Hell!" and in excruciating detail in Specifications of Material and Methods in Chapter Twenty One.

We average 17% of rent per property on Expenses or about $225 for an average four bedroom house. This is where many investors go wrong. They have a GM of $200 mo, project total expenses of $100 mo for a net of $100 mo. But their expenses will be $225 mo! With a GM of $200, they net negative $25 mo. What happens when you experience Tenant Turnover? Landlord out of business! Expenses include our maintenance/repair, administration expenses such as salaries, travel, phone, gas, office supplies, computers, education, food and our #1 enemy Tenant Turnover or vacancy.

10) STANDARDS, GOALS AND NORMATIVE CULTURE: This could be a fascinating chapter (or a book) by itself.

A) STANDARD: The least acceptable number or behavior within the company or group, below which you cannot go. Below which is failure. Below which you will be ostracized or fired. In some groups, physically beaten up. Or worse.

B) GOAL: The number or behavior to strive for, to shoot for. The hero striving for the Golden Fleece. Religion has saints. Sports has the Hall of Fame. Businesses only have money. Darn!

DHR uses Standard and Goal concepts in running our business. It defines what numbers are acceptable and what is not. You need to analyze your numbers, conclude they are possible, commit to reaching the Standard and striving for the Goal.

C) NORMATIVE CULTURE: All groups have a culture of standard behavior, if you fall below the standard you will be confronted and if it continues, ostracized, then evicted. All groups and relationships (wife and husband, landlord vs. tenant) have a leadership struggle, call it a "who's in control" fight. Paraphrasing Machiavelli, "The leader should be loved and feared. But if he is to choose one, it is to be feared." For more information, read Rod Hess's excellent book Normative Leadership.

11) CASH ON CASH %[7]: This is the one ratio you must understand, use and be successful at. It is powerful, simple and tells you everything! I love using it! I love striving for 100%. I love being at 100%.

12) 100% FINANCING: The Holy Grail of real estate financing. Essentially an extension of 100% Cash on Cash % but better**,** as you have NONE of your money in the deal, better yet, you take cash out of the deal!

There are many other ratios that are real estate useful. See <u>What Every Real Estate Investor Needs To Know About Cash Flow... and 36 Other Key Financial Measures</u> by Frank Gallinelli.

If you are successful with Cash on Cash % all the others fall into line - and look very good. I calculate this ratio as part of my Pre-Offer Property Worksheet. The ratio is a gold standard for real estate investments. It is so important I have devoted the entire Chapter 5, "The One Ratio To Die For", to it.

"THE DIFFERENCE BETWEEN AN INVESTOR AND A BUSINESSPERSON IS THAT AN INVESTOR MAKES AN INVESTMENT DECISION ONCE AND IF SUCCESSFUL, WITH LITTLE EFFORT THEREAFTER, RECEIVES ITS FINANCIAL REWARDS YEAR AFTER YEAR. THE BUSINESSPERSON NEVER STOPS WORKING."

The Investor's job is to allocate capital and receive a return on that capital, thus the much maligned term Capitalist. An Investor may use his own capital, other Investors' capital or borrowed capital. The Investor studies the market's opportunities and decides where to put his capital to work to obtain the best return. I measure this with my simple Cash on Cash % return although there are many other more sophisticated ratios and methods available.

A small businessperson runs a business to make a profit generally judged on a monthly, quarterly and annual basis. If the Small Businessperson becomes tired, ill, retires, the economy goes into a recession, the product is no longer competitive or an 800 lb gorilla enters the market, the businessperson must reinvent the business (if she has the energy and creativity) sell the business (if there is a market and if it has equity) or walk away. When the businessman stops, the money stops. Examples:

---

[7] The cash on cash % is explained in Chapter 5.

SELLING HOUSES: Realtor or Agent, one can, in good times, if you have talent, work hard and occupy a good niche, make large sums of money. As market conditions change, the money dries up and agents fall like leaves in Spring.

FLIPPING HOUSES: Quite the rage during the price run up of 2004 – 2007 but even then it wasn't easy – today nothing. Zilch. Or worse. Buy – Rehab – Hold – Discount – Hold – Discount – Loss.

MEDICAL COMPUTERS TO DOCTORS: Started this business in 1978, reinvented it multiple times, has provided a good living for our family, it is however, not saleable, has little equity, wife ran it from 1996 – 2010, son is current President, continuous struggle, survived because of its' narrow niche.

I would rather be an Investor than a Businessperson, wouldn't you? I may not be a Warren Buffett but I can allocate my limited capital and considerable sweat equity to buy, rehab and rent high-demand/low-supply 4/5 bedroom houses in good school districts to Section 8 tenants while continuing in student rentals and garages.

If the niche is strong and your offering amenity-rich, your turnover will be low, your rental business will evolve into an Investment, you being the Investor. I even like how it sounds.

References:

1. <u>Built to Last: Successful Habits of Visionary Companies</u>, Jim Collins and Jerry Porras. How to build a company.

2. <u>Do It</u>, John Roger and Peter McWilliams. Efficiency and effectiveness..

3. <u>Getting Things Done</u>, Edwin C. Bliss. Efficiency and effectiveness.

4. <u>Good to Great</u>, Jim Collins. The principles followed by great companies

5. <u>How to Win Friends And Influence People</u>, Dale Carnegie. Best book on human relations ever written.

6. <u>In Search of Excellence</u>, Thomas Peters and Robert Waterman. So much in 250 pages.

7. <u>Management and Machiavelli</u>, Anthony Jay. Basics of Power. Having, understanding and using power is core to running a business.

8. <u>Normative Leadership</u>, Rod Hess. RJ.hess@verizon.net or www.helpathy.com How all groups really work, written by a master

9. <u>Quality is Free</u>, Philip Crosby. Customer satisfaction is FREE!

10. <u>The Effective Executive</u>, Peter Drucker. An absolute must read. Genius.

11. <u>The Essays of Warren Buffet: Lessons For Corporate America</u>, Lawrence Cunningham. Lessons from the best Investor in the 20th Century.

12. <u>The Five Most Important Questions You Will Ever Ask Your Organization</u>, Peter Drucker. More genius.

13. <u>The One Minute Manager</u>, Kenneth Blanchard. Read it. Try it. It works.

14. <u>The Prince</u>, Niccolò Machiavelli. The first and still the best book on Power.

15. <u>The Snowball: Warren Buffet and the Business of Life</u>, Alice Schroeder. In real estate terminology - Compounding!

Chapter Five

The One Ratio to Die For

The Holy Grail: 100% Financing

Do you have a lot of Capital? I thought so. Me too. Capital, defined as your cash money not borrowed in any form, always seems to be in short supply. And unless I am very careful and disciplined, my capital can quickly disappear into the purchase and rehab of a rental house, leaving no capital for the purchase of the next opportunity.

Wall Street, in the Mergers and Acquisitions department, have "Deal Makers" who specialize in creating deals with good returns but using very little (or none!) of their own money. Their Net return on their own cash into the deal is infinite if their capital invested is zero! Very sweet. Sign me up.

Using "Other Peoples' Money" (OPM) is a cornerstone of real estate investing. Obtaining 100% financing, while still maintaining the GM and Net standards, is difficult but can be done. The books Nothing Down and Nothing Down for the 90s by Robert Allen were best sellers in the 1980's and 90's. Like many real estate gurus whose reign ended poorly, Allen declared bankruptcy in 1996. Allen's Nothing Down concept enabled a skilled practitioner in leverage to acquire properties but did not emphasize effective management focusing on a positive monthly Net.

In early 2009, I came across the Cash on Cash % Ratio, which is similar to Return on Investment (ROI). It was simple to calculate and if an investor was successful with this one Ratio, most other ratios would also be positive. Not being an accounting type I decided to concentrate on this Ratio.

One calculates it by adding all the costs associated with the house; i.e. purchase price, settlement costs, rehab and financing during the rehab to reach a TOTAL COST; from TOTAL COST subtract the loan amount (Principal) of your mortgage - this gives your CASH INVESTED; divide CASH INVESTED into ANNUAL NET= Cash on Cash % Ratio.

> Purchase Price +settlement + Rehab + financing during rehab = TOTAL COST
> TOTAL COST – loan amount= CASH INVESTED
> ANNUAL NET ÷ CASH INVESTED = Cash on Cash %

A good Wall Street bond return today is under 5%. The stock market, historically, has returned 8-10%. We aim for much higher returns. Next are three examples of possible returns.

Purchase Price	Settlements (2)	Rehab	Finance	Total Cost	Mortgage Principal	Cash Invested	Annual Net	CASH/ CASH %
40,000	5,000	25,000	1,500	71,500	65,000	(6,500)	3,000	46%
35,000	5,000	35,000	0	75,000	70,000	(5,000)	4,200	84%
52,000	5,000	20,000	0	72,000	75,000	+3,000	3,750	Infinite

What is the right Standard and Goal for the Cash on Cash % ? 25% is a great return but it takes 4 years to return your cash invested. Too long! 50% Cash on Cash takes two years. 75% takes one and a quarter years. 100% takes one year! All fantastic returns, which you then receive every year! Maintain a 93% occupancy rate and even at 25% you are investing in the upper echelons of world class.

My house purchases in 2010, averaged Cash on Cash % of 41%. In 2011 it was 94%. Not 100% but getting there. I'm learning. It's fun.

100% FINANCING is **CASH ON CASH %** on steroids. **100% FINANCING** means your TOTAL COST minus your MORTGAGE PRINCIPAL equals zero or if the MORTGAGE PRINCIPAL is the larger of the two, it means you took the difference out in cash (look at example #3 above). Both scenarios mean you have none of your own money into the house. In either circumstance you can merrily skip along the yellow brick road to find your next miracle house. Examples are below:

Basic Techniques for both 100% Cash on Cash and 100% Financing

A. **Control Your Purchase Price:** In my market I project an average purchase price for REO (Real Estate Owned) houses of $25,000 for a row/twin and $40,000 for a detached house. Total costs of the 2 settlements (1st is cash or borrowed money, 2nd is the after rehab permanent financing) about $5,000. For the purchase, use your own capital, such as saving account, IRA, 401K, or borrow from a spouse, relative, partner, buddy, Hard Money Lender, Home Equity Line of Credit, credit cards, or bank.

B. Control Your Rehab Costs: In my market I project an average rehab of $25,000. But it all depends on the condition of the house, it could be $35,000 or $15,000 or even less. Focus on segmenting and tracking the rehab costs on the "A" Pre Offer Property Worksheet. Hold the individual contractor specialist responsible for their contractual numbers. Send out the Contract Tracking form to all contractors weekly even if it's a zero. Make them aware that every dollar is being looked at.

C. Permanent Financing Terms, From Whom: In my market at this time, I project receiving permanent financing from a Commercial Bank with a 20 yr. amortization, 5 year balloon, 70% LTV at about 5% -7%. You have an A (for you) and B (for the bank) Pre Offer Property Worksheet which outlines the rehab costs. Using Funny Money[8], you increase the bank's rehab costs (on B) by 50% or 75% over your actual costs. The bank wants you to have cash invested in the project. That's understandable. You don't want to have cash invested in the project. That's understandable.

D. Appraisal time: Meet the appraiser, give him a packet with your (B) Pre Offer Property Worksheet. Have a lease, be it a real one or one the Tooth Fairy left under your pillow. Helps to have before rehab pictures, to point out the vast improvement the rehab made. We include three 8x10 glossy, 4 pictures per page, showing the nasty property before the rehab. Why? You are asking the appraiser and the bank to value a house at $100,000 that 90 days ago was sold to you at $35,000. Include recent favorable area sales and a letter outlining exactly what the rehab entailed; at the bottom of the letter include a slightly elevated estimate of what you think the house is worth. The appraiser may ignore your estimate but it can't hurt that she knows what you want.

---

[8] Funny Money is later explained in chapter 17.

E. An Example of the Holy Grail – 100% Financing

Purchase Price	Settlement (2)	Rehab	Total	Appraisal	LTV	Mortgage Loan Am't	Cash Out of Pocket
40,000	5,000	25,000	70,000	100,000	70%	70,000	0

Rent	PITI	GM	Expenses	Net	Annual Net	Cash on Cash %	100% Financing
1,300	800	500	221	279	3,348	Infinite	Yes

F. Real Life Financing Examples taken from Chapter Twenty

Chapter Twenty Property Number	Purchase Price	Settlement Costs (2)	Rehab Costs	Total Cost	Appraised Value	Mortgage Principal Loaned	Cash Out of Pocket	Annual Net	Cash on Cash % / 100% Financing
#44	$40,000	$3,581	$36,503	$80,084	$120,000	$71,000	(9,084)	$7,664	84% / No
#45	$19,000	$3,889	$42,859	$65,748	$129,000	$75,000	+9,252	$3,600	Infinite / Yes
#48	$35,000	$3,901	$45,604	$84,505	$110,000	$77,000	(7,505)	$4,200	56% / No

G. Let's go over the strategies again:

1) Invest your own cash or borrow short term for some or all of purchase price, settlement costs, rehab and financing costs during the rehab.

2) Commercial banks currently lend, as permanent financing, 70% of appraisal. You supply them or their appraiser with a packet including a Pre Offer Property Worksheet (B), letter of work done, your anticipated appraisal value, pictures of before rehab, favorable recent comparable sales and a current or soon-to-be lease.

3) Another option is to have the seller or realtor, or mother or friend, finance the purchase price for 60 - 120 days, during the rehab, then borrow with credit cards (or whatever) the rehab money, then have a commercial bank ready to take you out with a mortgage at 70% of appraised value, which will hopefully equal or even exceed your total cost and cash into the deal.

4) Another path is to have the FHA lend you 95% of purchase price as your primary residence. You then use credit cards (whatever) to finance the rehab, after which you go to a local credit union or bank and ask for a Home Equity Line of Credit based on the new after-rehab appraisal. This is very cheap money. I have a Home Equity Line of Credit (LOC) on my personal residence at 4%. I gaze fondly at and kiss the 4% monthly statement.

5) There are many ways to achieve 100% Cash on Cash % and 100% Financing. As market conditions change the methods change as well. Be creative. Figure one deal at a time.

6) **MORE FINANCING SCENARIOS**

1. 100% FINANCING

Purchase	Settlements (2)	Rehab	Total Costs	Permanent Financing Mortgage	Cash Invested	PITI	Rent	Gross Margin	Expenses 17%	Monthly Net	Annual Net	Cash on Cash %
$35K	$5K	$31K	$71K	$72K	+1000	$800	$1250	$450	$213	$237	$2,844	Infinite

How it was done. REO. Original asking price $68,000, DOM (Days on Market) 120, asking price at time of offer $52,000. First ridiculous offer $30,000. Negotiated to $35,000. Purchase price, settlement cost and rehab paid cash from an IRA. Commercial Bank appraises at $103,000 after rehab, lends 70%, at 7%, 20 yr. amortization, 5 yr. balloon. Section 8 Tenant, 4 bed, 1.5 ba. at $1,250 mo. You had no cash invested. You received $1000 at the 2nd settlement that gave you the permanent financing.

2. HOME EQUITY LINES OR 2ND MORTGAGES CAN CREATE 100% FINANCING

Purchase	Settlements (2)	Rehab	Total Costs	Mortgage 1st 65K 2nd 32K	Cash Invested	PITI w/ 1st & 2nd Mortgage	Rent	Gross Margin	Expenses 17%	Monthly Net	Annual Net	Cash on Cash %
$64K	$5K	$28K	$97K	65K 32K 97K	0	$940	$1275	$335	$217	$118	$1,416	Infinite

How it was done. REO. Original asking price $109,900. Asking price at time of offer $88,000. First ridiculous offer $50,000. Negotiated to $64,000. Primary mortgage FHA $65,000, 30 yr. 5.5%. Principal and Interest of 1st $320 mo, Home Equity of $32,000 loaned after rehab, appraised at $135K, 2nd mortgage at 4.5% over 10 yrs. This does not meet our GM and Net standard but a Cash on Cash% of infinity is excellent.

3. GOOD BUY, MAJOR REHAB, STUDENT RENTAL, 100% FINANCING

Purchase	Settlements (2)	Rehab	Total	Mortgage	Cash Invested	PITI	Rent	Gross Margin	Expenses 17%	Monthly Net	Annual Net	Cash on Cash %
$47K	$5K	$79K	$131K	$131K	0	$1300	$1900	$600	$323	$277	$3,324	Infinite

How it was done. REO, major problems need creative solution plus full rehab. Original asking price $119,900, asking price at time (DOM 145) of our offer $100,000. First ridiculous offer $40,000 negotiated to 47K. Wooded backyard looking down to a stream. Finished basement with 2 bedrooms and full bath, 2 decks overlooking rear, IRA financed purchase and rehab, commercial bank financed $131,000 at 20 years, 7%, 5 yr balloon. Student rental, 6 bedrooms, $320/bedroom, $1,900 mo.

No Money Down encompasses many different techniques. Essentially it means **Financing 100%** of the purchase price at the initial settlement, but a smart and bank-friendly method is to use your own capital or borrow short term from a hard money lender, equity line of credit or even credit cards for the purchase and rehab; then obtain permanent financing. Today, most of the time you need a commercial bank. The object of 100% financing is to have the permanent financing equal or exceed your TOTAL COSTS which are purchase price, rehab costs, financing and both settlements. That's **100% Financing**, and it's a beautiful thing.

Chapter Six

1st Wonderful Niche: Good School District

Buy Houses where Families want to Live

If you have kids, what is the first thing you decided when you were looking to buy or rent a house? The school district. You then found the right house in that school district. Simple as that.

I figured all tenants with children are certainly no different than you or me. So I researched the school districts in my county by searching on the internet "Pennsylvania SAT scores by School District". (You can Google your State and find tons of information on the internet.) I came across **http://www.scribd.com/doc/21687868/Pennsylvania-Public-Schools-SAT** and **http://www.publicschoolreview.com.** I found three school districts in my county had poor (under 900) and declining average SAT scores. This coincided with their poor reputation. I eliminated them. I determined that a "good" and acceptable SAT average was above 940. The websites also gave valuable information on the school district's population, age, average family size, minority population, average age of children, etc. I then searched the Multiple Listing Service (MLS) for pockets of low cost blue collar housing, perhaps row houses or twins, in the remaining good school districts. Within a few hours, I eliminated wealthy school districts which had an average house price between $379,000 and $405,000 and more importantly, I could not find pockets of low cost housing. I was left with five. Today all of my rentals are within those 5 good school districts.

So the logic is thus:

1) Houses in good school districts rent quickly since the demand is strong.

2) Tenants renting in good school districts will pay more and stay longer since their kids connect and make friends on the block, neighborhood and participate in school's teams and clubs.

3) Tenants in good school districts know their kids are getting a good education, are safe, and see a future for them. Therefore they don't want to move!

Now let's take a look at Tenant Turnover and why it's so very, very important to your bottom line. All my real estate books and courses, as well as what I learned speaking with experienced investors, conclude that Tenant Turnover is the number one expense. The staggering cost of Tenant Turnover is covered below. It's an eye opener. Scary too.

Tenant leaves or is evicted. Tenant Turnover Rehab (TTR) begins ASAP. Here is a list of average costs of rehabs.

1. Demo. Everything out. All rugs out. Landscape. ($200 - $500)

2. Dumpster Rental. ($0 - $500)

3. Painting entire property ($500 - $2,000)

4. Conversion to refinished hardwood floors, new quarter round. Ceramic tile elsewhere. Absolutely no carpets. ($1,500 - $2,500)

5. Change locks, new mini blinds, some new screens, clean, repair kitchen and bathrooms. ($200 - $750)

6. Repair/upgrade items as needed: 10 year Smoke Detectors, Pest Control, maintain and silvercoat flat roof, broken doors, stove, fan/light, plumbing and electrical. ($250 - $1,500)

7. Thorough cleaning ($50 - $300)

8. One to three months vacancy while paying PITI – ($800 – $2,400)

9. Marketing costs – ($50 – $300)

10. Precious Time, Energy, Gas, Part Time help – ($100 – $500)

TOTAL: $4,500 - $11,000. Believe it! It's why landlords go bankrupt.

Total costs will be MORE if you previously let in slobs. **STILL MORE** if you evict because during the lengthy eviction process, they sure as hell ain't paying rent and may trash the house.

My last eight Tenant Turnover Rehabs cost from $4,500 - $9,500. Because the cost is so high, it is important to implement The Eliminators! during the initial rehab. (explained in detail in chapter 16 and 21). A TTR will be $2,500 to $3,500 less if you have already implemented steps in chapters 16 and 21. Save yourself thousands. Follow my invaluable Specification for Methods and Materials in Chapter 21. A Rehab Bible.

Let's take a look at your average rental to see how long it takes you to earn back the money spent on a Tenant Turnover Rehab.

RENT	PITI		GM	EXPENSES	MO.NET		YR/NET
$1,275/mo	$800	=	$475/mo	$217/mo	$258	x12	$3,096

TENANT TURNOVER REHAB COSTS $4500- $11,000
ANNUAL NET $3,096 TAKES 1.5 – 3.5 YRS TO BREAK EVEN!

Tenant Turnover eliminates net profit! Years just to break even! This is very serious. This is why many landlords have no Net Income unless the mortgage is paid off. This is why we do niche rentals. We need the Supply/Demand fulcrum to work for us. We must cut down, as much as humanly possible, Tenant Turnover, the number one Landlord killer! And good school districts are your first step in this direction. But there are more steps in the forthcoming chapters. TEACHING POINT, SLUMLORDS: Yes Virginia, there are slumlords, and I have met a few. Best definition of a slumlord is a landlord who buys low in a ghetto and does not maintain his property. A few are wealthy because they are smart, ruthless and know exactly what they are doing. However I find most are "Accidental Slumlords" and barely survive financially. Their business evolved without a clear plan focusing on a profitable niche. It's difficult to maintain a property if you are losing money and dead broke. These "Accidental Slumlords" have 1 of the 25 three bedroom house rentals in the newspaper in a bad school district. They have a commodity no one wants.

I must admit, when I first started, I was almost enticed to buy cheap houses in a bad school district. They were so cheap anyone could make a ton of money, right? How could you lose? Thank goodness I didn't. Don't you do it. Buy in a good school district!

Chapter Seven

2nd Wonderful Niche: 4/5 Bedroom Houses

Amazing Bedroom Secrets Revealed!

This guy Max kept screaming, literally screaming, that he had doubled and tripled his houses Net income! I'm driving, excited, squirming, (like listening to my first Beatles record) breathing hard, front window fogging up, heart pounding like a jack hammer on steroids, I pull over, put my seat back, close my eyes, breathe in, then out, breathe in, then out, Max still screaming, "TRIPLE THE NET PROFIT AND WHOOPIE! INTO THE BANKAROO!"

I sit up, eyes wide open like high beams down a country road, hit replay to get the angle this clown was riding. Max says, his wife/bookkeeper casually asked him, while doing the dishes, why his 4 bedrooms had $200 a month higher Net profit, less turnover, and longer tenant stay while PITI and expenses was the same as his three bedrooms. Max screamed, "SCREW 3 BEDROOMS! FOUR, FIVE OR NOTHING!" Max converted his basements, front and rear porches or open floor spaces to four and sometimes five bedrooms.

I wiped off the front window and drove to a 3 bedroom I was rehabbing and "found" the 4th bedroom in the rear porch. Wham! $200 to the bottom line! I ran down the block and knocked on the door of a current three bedroom house I owned. WHAM! I had a 4th bedroom in the basement waiting like a present on Christmas day! I was dazed and had to sit down on the curb. Was this true? Was it all a dream? I felt like I was a 49er at Sutter's Mill during the California gold rush and just hit a vein of pure yellow! This made sense. Money sense. But only if there was strong demand. I needed to verify the demand.

I looked in our local paper and Craigslist (you should do the same) for four/five bedroom houses with moderate rents ($1,200- $1,600 mo) in good school districts. I found two. But there were 12 three-bedroom houses for rent. I placed similar, but separate house rental ads for three, four and five bedrooms in the paper and Craigslist. First day I received four calls for the four-bedroom and two calls each for the three and five. The second day, three calls for the four and one each for the three and five. The numbers spoke loudly but what resonated like a hand reaching through the phone and grabbing my throat was the **URGENCY** of the callers for the four or five-bedrooms to **SEE THE HOUSE NOW!** Two remarked they had been looking unsuccessfully for months. One said she had been living for a year in a three-bedroom because she couldn't find an acceptable four-bedroom on the previous search. This was more than interesting; this was exciting! I have since confirmed that the demand for four and five bedroom houses in good school districts is much stronger than for two or three bedroom houses. Put an ad in the paper and Craigslist (or whatever advertising mediums dominate your area) and see what happens. Right to your cell phone. You will feel the demand or lack of it.

I decided to buy only three-bedroom houses which could be converted to a four/five, buy a four-bedroom to be rented as such or be converted into a five, or buy a straight five-bedroom. Six bedrooms are usually old, large and meandering, perfect for students.

Let's get a quick college degree in 'finding' or converting space to bedrooms. But first what qualifies, by code, as a bedroom?

WHAT IS A BEDROOM?

According to the 2009 International Residential Code[9] a bedroom must have:

A. 70 square feet, with the width or the length not less than 7 feet.

B. Must have egress (exit out of the building) - door or an egress window which must have a minimum of 5.7 square feet and start no more than 44 inches from the floor. Each municipality seems to interpret the 5.7 sq ft differently, so check with them.

C. The ceiling must be 7 feet or higher. If lower, as in an attic, the 70 sq ft must come from space directly under 5 ft or above of ceiling to floor measurement.

D. Heat

---

[9] I highly recommend owning this for reference to what the codes actually are, not what the inspector says they are.

LET'S COMPARE THE PROFIT OF A 3-4-5 BEDROOM RENTAL

	RENT	- PI	- TAXES	- INS	= GROSS MARGIN	- EXPENSES	= MO x12 NET	ANN NET
3 bed	$1,050/mo	- $560	- $200	- $40	= $250	- $173/mo	$77	$924
4 bed	$1.250/mo	- $560	- $210	- $45	= $435	- $213/mo	$222	$2,664 (188% ↑)
5 bed	$1,450/mo	- $600	- $230	- $50	= $570	- $247/mo	$323	$3,888 (46% ↑)

188% HIGHER NET CONVERTING A THREE TO A FOUR-BEDROOM!

46% HIGHER NET CONVERTING A FOUR TO A FIVE-BEDROOM!

Yes, a four-bedroom nets 188% more than a three-bedroom, has higher demand, less turnover and a longer tenant stay. The conversion cost is approximately $2,500 for a back/front porch or other room/space and $4,000 to $6,000 for a basement conversion to a fourth bedroom, plus a den, and a powder room (another $2500- $3,000). These costs, done during the original rehab, and before a permanent mortgage is placed, can with some skill and luck be financed over the amortization schedule of the mortgage. Let's say the 4th bedroom conversion cost is $3,000. Financed, that's $24 a month over 20 years. If $5,000 it's $40 a month. If $10,000 it's $80 a month. But, you increase your rent by a multiple of that, making your gross margin and net significantly higher. More than just interesting isn't it? I'm sure you can see why I own the following:

OF THE 62 HOUSES I HAVE

THREE-BEDROOM	**5**	**8%**
FOUR-BEDROOM	**36**	**58%**
FIVE-BEDROOM	**17**	**27%**
SIX-BEDROOM[10]	**4**	**7%**

The additional net of each 4/5/6 bedroom makes the entire difference in having an Investor happily stuffing his pockets or struggling for gas money. Find a niche and be good at it!

---

[10] For student rentals, I rehab into six bedrooms with 2 full baths. Three of the four 6-bedroom houses are student rentals.

Chapter Eight

3rd Wonderful Niche: Section 8 Housing

The Fed Pays the Rent

After two and a half years of trying to be a successful landlord, during the summer of 2007, I suffered through six very expensive tenant turnovers. These turnovers eliminated profit for those houses for years to come. Three of the tenants left voluntarily and three were evicted. However, of the six turnovers, five were cash tenants, but at that time my tenants were about 50% Section 8 and 50% Cash. I researched for previous Section 8 tenant turnovers and I found a few but they were caused by poor tenant choice[11], made before I implemented the rigorous screening procedures centered on the Home Visit. Other than these self-inflicted wounds, my four/five bedroom Section 8 tenants had NO TURNOVERS. Epiphany! The decision was made that all new tenants would be well-screened Section 8 tenants.

Section 8 tenant demand for four and five-bedroom houses in good school districts is substantial. I am patient and always complete a Home Visit. We find 33% of our prospective applicants will not allow us in for the Home Visit; another 33% fail the Home Visit. For the 33% that do pass, we then have an on-line eviction/credit/criminal check, and also speak with current and past landlords. Some prospects who are approved have not obtained a Landlord Lease Packet and can't move for 90 days. I keep scheduling open houses and processing applications until I find the right one who can move in now! As I write this, Tenant Turnover has slowed to a crawl and I am 100% rented.

---

[11] I go into detail about tenant choice and management in chapter 15

The Tenant Pays their Share

Section 8 pays an average of about 75% of the total rent although it varies greatly from tenant to tenant according to their income. Section 8 calculates how much the tenant is responsible for, and Section 8 pays the remainder.

The tenant pays their share in order to stay in the Section 8 program. If we have not received the rent by the 5th we mail a NOTICE OF NON-PAYMENT AND LATE CHARGE. On the 8th we mail a PAY OR MOVE notice. On the 12th we file in District Court. Within ten days, we are in court, gain a judgment, copy to caseworker and Director of Section 8. A lot of pressure to pay.

Section 8 Tenants, rightly so, feel that they won the Housing Lottery. They like our house, its amenities, the school district and they don't want to lose it. So they pay.

Rent Compounded 2.5% every year is HUGE!

Compounding is the secret to SLOWLY increasing your monthly Net. Section 8 sometimes allows an annual 2.5% rent adjustment. If we don't receive it, we fight for it. Makes an enormous difference over 3 or 5 or 10 years as our chart below shows.

No 2.5% annual raise? You are going backwards. Taxes and expenses (perhaps insurance) may increase. But the principal and interest payment stays the same and there lies one of our secret weapons.

The following table includes a 2.5% annual rent adjustment (starting at $1,250 mo for a four bedroom house), principal/interest holding steady at $560, and a 2.5% increase in taxes, insurance (hope not) and expenses (hope not). I fight to keep my expenses below 17% of the rent.

	RENTAL PRICE	RENT ADJ 2.5%	NEW RENT		P&I	TAXES Increase 2.5%	INS Increase 2.5%	EXPENSES 2.5%	TOTAL PAYOUTS		MO NET	ANNUAL NET
Yr 1	$ 1,250	$ 31	$ 1,281	-	$ 560	$ 200	$ 40	$ 212	$ 1,012	=	$ 238	$ 2,856
Yr 2	$ 1,281	$ 32	$ 1,313	-	$ 560	$ 205	$ 41	$ 217	$ 1,024	=	$ 257	$ 3,084
Yr 3	$ 1,313	$ 33	$ 1,346	-	$ 560	$ 210	$ 42	$ 223	$ 1,041	=	$ 272	$ 3,264
Yr 4	$ 1,346	$ 34	$ 1,380	-	$ 560	$ 215	$ 43	$ 229	$ 1,047	=	$ 299	$ 3,588
Yr 5	$ 1,380	$ 34	$ 1,414	-	$ 560	$ 221	$ 44	$ 235	$ 1,057	=	$ 323	$ 3,876
Yr 6	$ 1,414	$ 35	$ 1,449	-	$ 560	$ 226	$ 45	$ 240	$ 1,071	=	$ 343	$ 4,111

	RENTAL PRICE	RENT ADJ 2.5%	NEW RENT		P&I	TAXES Increase 2.5%	INS Increase 2.5%	EXPEN SES 2.5%	TOTAL PAYOUTS		MO NET	ANNUAL NET
Yr 7	$ 1,449	$ 36	$ 1,485	-	$ 560	$ 232	$ 46	$ 246	$ 1,086	=	$ 363	$ 4,352
Yr 8	$ 1,485	$ 37	$ 1,522	-	$ 560	$ 238	$ 48	$ 252	$ 1,098	=	$ 387	$ 4,644
Yr 9	$ 1,522	$ 38	$ 1,560	-	$ 560	$ 244	$ 49	$ 259	$ 1,112	=	$ 410	$ 4,920
Yr 10	$ 1,560	$ 39	$ 1,599	-	$ 560	$ 250	$ 50	$ 265	$ 1,125	=	$ 435	$ 5,220

AFTER 10 YEARS YOU HAVE INCREASED YOUR MONTHLY AND ANNUAL NET BY

83 %!

The magic of Compounding. Even at 2.5%!

THE BASICS OF SECTION 8 HOUSING

The Reputation

Section 8 Housing has, in some circles, a dirt ball reputation. Section 8 tenants are slobs, destroy houses, schools, and neighborhoods and are routinely involved with guns, drugs and jail. Just the type of people **NOT** to build a business around! But let's take a deeper look...

The TRI-Relationships

Section 8 Housing, under Housing and Urban Development (HUD), has its own contract, Housing Assistance Payments (HAP) for the Landlord and Tenant to sign. This is a triangular relationship between (1) Tenant and Landlord (Tenant signs Landlord's lease), (2) Tenant and Section 8 (Tenant signs HUD's HAP contract) and (3) Landlord and Section 8 (Landlord signs HUD's HAP contract).

Bureaucratic Rules Rule

Section 8 is a multi-billion dollar Federal government bureaucratic quagmire which failed in its initial attempt to directly house the nation's poor (Remember the Projects? High Rise apartment complexes filled with Crime, Fear, Poverty, Gangs, etc. That was HUD. A legendary disaster.) After numerous sensational exposés, HUD blew up (literally) the Projects. HUD now administers the Section 8 Tenants program but wisely uses Private Investors as Landlords.

"WASHINGTON, WE HAVE A PROBLEM!"

Can you imagine private, independent, investor entrepreneurs interacting with government rule-oriented, paper pushing, salaried, control freak minions? Sounds like a lot of fun. Some landlords try, become frustrated and opt out. Others won't even try.

But it's like being in the Army. The game is to learn their rules, their methods, and discipline yourself to adhere to them, so they don't have the opportunity to give you a hard time. If you fight the rules, you lose. Time and energy are money, finite and disappearing every second. You win by having the discipline to do what they want you to do.

If, however, an issue is important (money) and they are clearly wrong, ACCORDING TO THEIR RULES (I have the HUD Section 8 Manual and so should you) then go to war. I have, several times. But How to Win Friends and Influence People (great book by Dale Carnegie) wins more over time. Section 8 Caseworkers and the local Section 8 Director respect a good landlord who has good, clean properties, does repairs promptly and passes inspections. The tenants will help by passing on their positive opinions to their Caseworker and the Director.

DEFINITION OF TERMS FOR SECTION 8 HOUSING

The following are some of the basic Section 8 rules to understand and follow:

1. **TENANT**: A prospective tenant applies for Section 8. Their income is below certain standards. The tenant is put on a waiting list. Years pass. Eventually they are called and must pass a drug test, criminal check, eviction check, and be employed, even if marginally. I have found, because of this screening, Section 8 tenants are not the bottom of the barrel. Yes, some bad ones slip through, but it's limited. We run our own credit check, criminal check, eviction check (all three, 10 minutes, Landlord website, $25) and most important of all, our Tenant Home Visit. (See Chapter 15, Tenant Choice and Management.) Don't fret bad credit since Section 8 pays most of the rent with the tenant paying according to his or her income. They are also under pressure from Section 8 to pay their share of the rent if she wants to stay in the program. It's effective. I have found that Section 8 tenants do pay their assigned share.

2. **VOUCHER**: Once approved the tenant receives a voucher with the approved number of bedrooms and dates the voucher is valid for. We ask to see the

voucher to check both. Section 8 pays according to the number of bedrooms. Period. A tenant with a three-bedroom voucher may say, "My caseworker says I can rent a four-bedroom." Yes, a three-bedroom voucher can rent a four-bedroom, but the landlord will receive three-bedroom rent. Therefore a four-bedroom voucher rents our four-bedroom house. A five-bedroom voucher rents our five-bedroom house.

3. **CERTIFIED LETTER/60-DAY NOTICE**: When a tenant wants to move they must give their current landlord 60 days notice by certified mail. The 60 days start from the date of the certified letter.

Section 8 tenants learn the following mantras in Tenant School.

"My landlord said I can move any time."

"I told my landlord months ago."

"I don't want to send the letter 'til I find a place."

"I have an emergency and can move any time I find a house."

> NO. NO. NO. NO. Certified letter starts the 60 days notice. We process tenants that can't move until the 1st of the month following the expiration of 60 days, but we realize that's out 70-90 plus days. We and you want to rent NOW!

4. **LANDLORD RELEASE LETTER TO SECTION 8:** The landlord, once they receive the 60-Day notice, must visit the property to assess any tenant damage, which if there is, tenant must pay before moving. Landlord then writes a release letter to Section 8 saying the tenant doesn't owe money, there is no damage and they are free to move after the 60 days.

5. **LANDLORD LEASE PACKET:** Ask all Section 8 tenants at an Open House: "Do you have a Landlord Lease Packet?" Ask prospective tenants on the phone, "Do you have a Landlord Lease Packet?" If they do they are ready to move! Once Section 8 receives the landlord's release letter they issue a Landlord Lease Packet, which has various forms and the HAP contract for the new landlord to fill out and sign.

So you now have the Landlord Lease Packet!

A) Enclose a Settlement sheet proving you own the property.

B) Enclose a Certificate of Occupancy (CO) from the municipality. The CO is issued after that municipality inspects and passes your property. Each municipality has a different name for the CO, such as Rental License, Certificate of Occupancy, Occupancy Permit etc.

C) Landlord includes three copies of Landlord's Lease which he signs. One for Section 8, one for the tenant, one to be mailed back to the landlord after tenant signs and Section 8 approves all paperwork and the rental amount.

D) Landlord fills out HAP contract pages

E) Landlord gives completed Lease Packet to the tenant.

F) Tenant makes appointment with Section 8 caseworker, tenant signs HAP contract, rental amount is approved or rejected by the Section 8 caseworker. If rejected (always too high!) caseworker calls landlord and negotiates according to a Double Secret quantum formula, the original copy, handwritten during a 47-day desert fast by I HUD in 1887, stored in the same bank vault as The Secret Coke Formula and the Virgin Mary's letter to the Three Children of Fatima.

G) If the rental amount is changed, landlord must initial the change.

6. **10th OF THE MONTH:** The tenant hand carries the Landlord Lease Packet to an appointment (above) which must occur by the 10th of the month for the tenant to move into your house on the 1st of the following month. That's the 10th of the month! Not the 11th or 12th. Why? If it's past the 10th you wait one more month to rent and receive payment. (Yes, lots of Rules!) Obviously the caseworkers are busy on the 10th and you sometimes must perform triple jointed miracles to make the 10th happen.

7. **SECTION 8 INSPECTION:** It's not over yet! Section 8, once they approve your Lease Packet and rent amount, the caseworker schedules an inspection

ASAP but definitely before the 31st. Tenant cannot move in (i.e. no rental payment) until house passes the Inspection. The inspection game is similar to "Grand Theft Auto," but called "Break Landlord's Balls." If one totally immaterial item fails (screen is torn, receptacle loose, bedroom door doesn't click shut), the house fails, item must be repaired and re-inspected before tenant moves in. Wonderful, isn't it?

Before the inspection, I send an experienced handyman through the house with our Inspection Check List form. Handyman then meets the Inspector with pad and smile. Writes down any deficiencies (don't wait for mailed copy); Handyman corrects them on the spot or the same day if possible. I call the caseworker for another inspection. Remember, tenant can't move in and you aren't paid 'til the date of the passed Inspection!

8. MOVE IN: Once inspection is passed, meet with tenant, preferably at the new home, complete lease, parts 2-7, and collect remainder of the security deposit. Do a walk through, and have tenant fill out Part 4 Tenant Move In/Move Out form. We have a lot of welcome gifts for the new tenant, as it sets a nice tone. Then give them the key! The tenant is excited! Their dream home!

Chapter Nine

4th Wonderful Niche: Garages

I am brilliant! Have a Wharton MBA! Thought of, planned out in minute detail, then implemented with military precision the Garage Niche! Fool ya? No. OK. Here's how it really happened.

One of my houses had a detached garage in the back of the lot on an alleyway. The garage was 20' deep by 20' wide, split down the middle by a plywood wall, with each side having its own 8' x 9' door. I used one side for my rehabs, the other was empty.

Billy, an electrician, met me at the garage one late afternoon to pick up a check. He pointed at the empty half.

"Using that side?"

"Nope."

"No one renting it?"

"Nope."

"Want to rent it?"

"Sure." Starting to catch the drift.

"How much?"

Didn't have a clue. $50 per mo? $75? More? I looked at Billy. He looked at me.

"I pay $110.00 in Chester (war zone) but don't go after dark. This here is nice." He looked around then back to me.

Tick. Tick. Tick. Have to say something. "How's $150?"

"Any security payment?" He reached into the shirt pocket of his red and black wool jacket and took out a checkbook.

"One month."

"So $300."

"Yeah."

He handed me the check, but somehow I was skeptical. I looked at it carefully, made out okay, was signed, yep $300. "Thanks Billy." I turned to leave.

"Joe, two things." Bad news coming. I knew it. Too good to last, "Need a key and where to send the checks."

I gave him a key and my business card with the PO Box.

He pointed down the alley at another garage. "That's yours too?"

"Tan stucco one, yes."

"You know Stan, the night Security Guard who lives across from it?"

"Young guy. About 30?"

"He's an auto mechanic looking for a shop. Might knock on his door." I was running late, so I didn't follow up. Anyway, lightening doesn't strike twice.

Next day my cell phone rang. "This is Stan. Billy said you might rent the garage. Didn't know how much?"

"Well… I… don't know." It was a double, about 20' deep, but 24' wide, poor condition.

"Got $10,000 of tools. Hafta make sure she's secure, you know, box out the windows and door, two padlocks on the rollup, paint, PECO for electric, panel, lights, receptacles, the whole nine yards."

Must be at least $3,000 in work he's talking about.

"You've seen inside Stan?" Old, dirty, wet when it rained.

"100 times as a kid. Used to play in it."

"So you know it's—"

"Roof too. Leaks."

"Stan I don't have the money to lay out right—"

"You mean the work? I'm doing the work."

"The materials."

"On me. Cost ya nuthing."

"OK."

"So how much? If it's too much, forget it. I'm small shop."

OK Joe, he's doing all the work, lives across the street, going to stay. Move him in NOW!.

"$200."

"OK. Thought it might be more. When can I start the work?"

"I'll need a check."

"OK if I pay three months up front? My bookkeeping ain't the best.""

"Month's security."

"So $800."

"Right. You there this afternoon, Stan?"

"Till four."

"I'll stop over."

Miracles happen. Not often, but garages qualify. Both of these tenants are still with me, paying every month.

I love garages. Houses versus Garages. Who wins:

	House	**Garage**
COST	$50,000 plus	Comes *free* with the house
MAINTENANCE	Maintenance requests, wear and tear, usually something.	*Zero (almost)*
TAXES	High, going higher, government rents you your land/ house	*Zero*
INSURANCE	Liability, Fire, Blanket coverage	*Zero*
EXIT	Eviction, court, turnover very expensive	*15 days late, change the locks and sell the goods*

AFTER RENTING THE FIRST TWO GARAGES, I WENT ON A CAMPAIGN!

1. Rented other garages I already owned.
2. Put a clause into my Residential Lease that the garage is to be rented separately.
3. Found a garage lease, altered it to resemble a life threatening steel trap.
4. Started to include the expected garage rental (if there was a garage) into the Pre Offer Property Worksheet to calculate the Net of prospective purchases.
5. Bought houses with garages, when available.

FINDING HOUSES WITH GARAGES

1. I don't buy garages. They come with the house, usually in the back of the lot. I did build three garages (see PAINFUL MISTAKE #3) but please don't do that.

2. The garage may be in poor condition. Doesn't matter. It's simple to rehab and maintain a garage. (See Specification)

3. I don't, and my real estate agents don't, specifically look for houses with garages. We look for houses that meet our criteria. But when we find a good house with a garage, we jump on it. Both feet. Single garage, good. Double, better. Big double, better still. Two garages. Six garages? Yes, one of my houses came with six garages. An estate sale. Big dilapidated stand alone four-bedroom house with six garages. WOW! When I first saw it, felt like I was fifteen ogling tanned skin moving in a white bikini that smiled and waved.

4. Sellers generally don't ask more (or not much more) for a house with a garage. Or three garages. Or six garages. It's an amenity like central air, finished basement, fenced in backyard etc. Nice, but part of the package.

5. Other investors generally don't appreciate the dramatic increase in Net and therefore don't bid higher for a house with a garage.

6. Realtor.com and Zillow.com give info if a house has a garage, if it's single or double. Make sure your realtors know you really, really like garages.

7. When you first discover a three-bedroom, potential for a fourth, with a garage, run out and see it, quickly work up a Pre Offer Property Worksheet for the numbers. If the Net is good, make an offer immediately. I do not offer more money for a house with a garage. But if there is a negotiation, it is a factor and I will pay $1,000 or $2,000 more. You can pay a little more knowing you will get back a lot, every month, every year.

WHAT $1,000/$2,000 MORE FOR A HOUSE WITH A GARAGE COSTS

Additional Cost	Interest Rate	Monthly Payment	Amortization Schedule	After 20 years
$1,000	7.50%	$8	20 yrs	$0
$2,000	7.50%	$16	20 yrs	$0

WHAT TO CHARGE FOR A GARAGE RENTAL

Price varies by geography and location. Look in the local paper and Craigslist. Go see five garages for rent. Owner may ask you to drive by first, as we do. That's OK. You learn about each neighborhood, block, and see the garage's condition and size. Bring tape and measure the garages (always have tape measure/flashlight in car 24/7). Bypass garages in "War Zones". That's not our market. Rental prices depend on location, security, size, electrical availability, front apron size, ceiling height, and loft. Ask the owner on the phone or in person about the previously mentioned amenities.

Single - approximately 10/12' x 18/22'	$125-$150-$175 per month
Double - approximately 20/23' x 20/25'	$235-$310 per month
Large- approximately 24'x35', 10' doors, 16' ceiling height, electric	$500 per month

---

PAINFUL MISTAKE #3
DON'T BUILD GARAGES

I was so enthusiastic about garages, I built three in the rear of lots of houses I owned. Purchased three 24' by 35' steel garage kits, put in 12' concrete apron, brought in electric, specifically built for contractors. After two frustrating years I finally got them built but it cost three times my estimated budget. Then a major recession. Contractors tank. Rented for 65% ($500 mo) of projected $750. But they did rent. And over time, it will be a decent investment. But the Cash on Cash% is far below my 25% Standard and therefore I won't do it again.

GARAGE RENTERS ARE:
1. Thirty-something to Middle-aged plus males with a love object car, motorcycle, boat or airplane. (Yes, we store one small airplane.)
2. Contractors of all kinds. They need the larger garages. Almost all need electric. A twelve foot cement apron in front of garage helps.

GARAGE RENTERS WANT, IN ORDER OF IMPORTANCE:
1. Near their home.
2. Safe area. Not a problem since we buy in only good school districts.

3. Secure garage. I eliminate any windows or regular walk-through entrance doors. Only one way in. Put two large slide locks with two special padlocks that can't be cut off on the roll-up garage door entrance.

4. Electric. Contractors want electric, lighting and receptacles. Costs about $1,000-$1,500 for the panel, lighting, electrician and electric company. Call the electric company to start the ball rolling. They want the business.

5. Garage renters rarely move. They pay. They have no option. It's a commercial not a residential lease. There's no legal/court protection. After fifteen days I'll change the locks, mail them notification of such and see what happens. They generally call me with a solution, which is money.

HOW TO ADVERTISE AND RENT A GARAGE:

1. Put three-line ad under storage/garages in the local paper and let it run two weeks at a time. Put an expanded ad on Craigslist at least three times a week. Craigslist is free. Examples:

    a. TOWN, 10' x 20' brick garage, safe, secure, storage, elec avail $150 mo. Joe 610-xxx-xxxx

    b. TOWN, 20' x 20', next to Police Station, secure, storage, $235 mo. Joe 610-xxx-xxxx

    c. TOWN, 24' x 35' for contractors, all steel, Elect, two 10' x 10' doors, 16' apex, 12' cement front apron, safe, secure, $500 mo. Joe 610-xxx-xxxx

2. Field phone calls, give them the address and ask them to ride by and, if interested, call back for an appointment. Don't try to meet them all. Most won't show up. Write down name and number of "hot" prospects who need a garage "TODAY," ask what they want it for. Storage of vintage cars is the #1 winner. Be friendly.

3. The tire kickers are those who want to start a business, mostly car repair. Stay away from "start ups." Ask them for first month's rent plus three months security on an annual lease. They go away.

4. "Hot Prospect" calls back, seemingly ready to go. Ask if he's ready to rent. Make an appointment. Request he call 60 minutes before, just to make sure it's a go. Some "Hot Prospects" don't call. You don't go because they won't be there.

5. "Hot Prospect" does call back, you show garage, tout attributes, tell him others are calling. I assess prospects by their appearance, manner, what they are driving (has a friend brought them?), lack of cell phone (no cell in today's world?) or what their storage use is. I may decide I don't want them. But in general it's a go. Then I attempt to close the sale. I am direct. "Do you want to rent it?" "When do you want to move in?"

6. I have a lease on a clipboard, a pen and a key. I fill out the single-sided one page draconian lease, ask them to sign it, get a check for first month's rent and security deposit and give them a key (if I have questions about them, no key until I run a credit, eviction and criminal check and their check clears). Sometimes, that's the last I hear from them. I even forget what a few of the garage renters look like. I hope it stays that way.

Don't forget NICE. They get Christmas cards with $10 Walmart gift card, birthday card and an Anniversary card with $10 or $20 gift card depending how long they have been with me.

We send a monthly statement to garage tenants as well as house tenants. Late fees are $50-$100 (depending on garage rent) for rent postmarked after the 3rd, another $25-$50 after the 10th, after the 20th it's $10 a day. If not paid and no word, I can change the locks after the 15th. I don't chase rent on the phone.

I have changed locks on a number of garage tenants who, in retrospect, I should not have rented to. I do nothing less than a one-year lease. Storing "between moves" or any temporary storage for "4-5 months" is rejected.

HOW TO REHAB A GARAGE

1. Outside: If stucco/aluminum siding we repair, prepare, prime, paint Toasted Almond. If brick we point if necessary. If vinyl or steel, nothing.

2. Roof: If shingles we repair with muck or possibly replace single shingles. I don't care what it looks like as long as it doesn't leak. Most of our garage roofs are flat. We torch down a rubber roof if necessary and silver coat every 5 years or so.

3. Inside: We box out all windows and the walk-in entrance door. We take everything out of the garage. Clean it. Repair, prepare and spray the walls and ceilings with

Zinsser Bullseye 123. Paint the cement floor, (I use Behr Slate Grey). Looks neat and clean. Ready to rent.

4. Roll up garage door: Buy a good one. Must be installed by a mechanic who really knows how. It's a tricky install to get the balance and fit right. Two special padlocks on commercial grade slide locks on the outside. One key.

HOW A GARAGE AFFECTS THE GROSS MARGIN AND NET
SIT DOWN. STAY CALM. NO SCREAMING!

A) HOUSE WITHOUT A GARAGE

HOUSE RENTAL	PITI	GROSS MARGIN	EXPENSES 17%	MONTHLY NET	ANNUAL NET
$1,250/mo -	$800 =	$450mo -	$213/mo =	$237	$2,844

B) HOUSE WITH A SINGLE GARAGE

HOUSE RENTAL	GARAGE RENTAL	TOTAL	PITI	GROSS MARGIN	EXPENSES	MONTHLY NET	ANNUAL NET
$1,250/mo +	$150 =	$1,400 -	$800 =	$600mo -	$221/mo =	$379	$4,548
				33%		59%	59%
				Higher!		Higher!	Higher!

C) HOUSE WITH A DOUBLE GARAGE

HOUSE RENTAL	GARAGE RENTAL	TOTAL	PITI	GROSS MARGIN	EXPENSES	MONTHLY NET	ANNUAL NET
$1,250/mo +	$250 =	$1,500 -	$800 =	$700mo -	$221/mo =	$479	$5,748
				55%		102%	102%
				Higher!		Higher!	Higher!

59% NET INCREASE FOR A SINGLE GARAGE

102% NET INCREASE FOR A DOUBLE GARAGE

I have 21 garages which bring me over $4,000 a month, which goes directly to the bottom line. Of my $22,000 a month Net Income, $4,000 of that comes from my 21 beautiful, gorgeous, no purchase cost, no maintenance, no taxes, no insurance, no hassle, no phone calls garages.

"Yes, Virginia, there is a Santa Claus. And if you are lucky he brings garages."

Double Garage, Electric, 250 per month

Seller considered this a knock down. Has upper level, 350 per month

90 years old, UGLY, but a beautiful 150 a mo. per side

5 Single beauties, double garage in rear, total over 1000 per month

Chapter Ten

5th Wonderful Niche: Student Housing

"Do you allow students?" College kid, Italian, three days growth.

"Sure. Where you from?"

"Concord University, just up the road in town."

"Pass it every day on Atlanta Road." Third group of students from Concord at this Open House.

"OK if we look around?" Three other acceptably sloppy guys with him, he's the leader.

"Sure. Basement is finished with two bedrooms, second bathroom. Back deck is big. Nice yard. Gas Heat."

They are back in ten minutes, excited.

"The ad said five bedrooms?"

"Last room before the deck. It's small."

"So is Charley and he's not here." They laugh. "Is there an application?"

"Yes but the application's not really meant for students. I'll take everyone's information. When do you want to move in?" (I now have a completely different application for students. Altered the Lease too.)

"Is July 15th OK?" they ask. I knew school started August 10th but wanted them in ASAP.

"July 1st", I say. "We start the lease on the first."

He looked around at the others. Heads nodded.

"OK. How much to move in?"

"$1,500 1st month's rent. $1,500 Security Deposit. So $3,000."

"And the electric and gas . . . "

"Tenants pay all utilities. You'll be responsible for the grass, snow, garbage and upkeep."

"But if something breaks you fix it?"

"Yes, but we'll go over all that when we get to the lease."

I take their names, addresses, Social Security numbers, drivers license numbers, date of birth and cell phone numbers. Also I ask for their parents' names, addresses, whether they own or rent, and all their phone numbers. All the other application stuff doesn't really apply to students. They don't have much if any credit or income. We make an appointment in three days to show Charley. I tell them to bring a check and if they are accepted we'll sign a lease. They leave smiling, chatting. I like them. They are on the Soccer Team and hope to win the conference championship.

Student Housing? I know zilch. Yes, the usual horror stories and what I remember as a student. I know that some investors specialize in Student Housing. It's developed into a . . . niche!

Concord University is two miles from my home with an expanding student enrollment. I'm familiar with the campus and quality of kids. But I need the nuts and bolts of Student Housing info. Amazon has three used books on the subject, so I buy all three. I call an investor who does student rentals in Philadelphia, a referral from a banker. He's very positive. "From year to year, they rent themselves. I have them sign a lease but that's about it. They're not demanding. In fact, sometimes I don't hear from the male students all year."

While I wait for the books, I visit the Housing Director at Concord University. He's young, friendly and has a problem.

"Simply put, it's supply and demand. We have five residential dormitories on campus," he shakes his head. "The area is full of houses built in the 50's, 60's and 70's that are too expensive to be rentals. No inexpensive older twins or rows. Housing is a continuous problem."

"What are students looking for? What do they want?"

"A location close to campus. The closer, the better. Everything else is secondary. Should be clean, decent, of course."

"What's close? One mile, two?"

"Best is walking distance but they do have cars. So one to two miles is close. Over that it lowers the price. But we have some as far as 8 miles."

"What's the price range? How do you determine it?"

"It's simple. $250 to $400 per bedroom per month. Closer to campus, more demand, higher the rent. Of course space and amenities play a part."

Later, I worked the numbers at $300 a bedroom. Then $325. The game seemed to be, buy large rundown houses within two miles of campus, then rehab for bedrooms.

I read the Student Housing books and spoke with a second Student Rental Investor. According to both sources, student rentals have a better Net than my four/five bedroom houses. My last eight four/five bedroom houses averaged $325 Net per month or $3,900 per year. As a goal, I'd like Student Housing to be. . . 50% higher! Plan: Buy cheap less than two miles from campus, find and convert to six bedrooms, two bathrooms, adequate parking. Six bedrooms at $320 is $1,920 a month. About $475 Net per month. Challenge is finding inexpensive houses ($50,000–$100,000), with potential for six bedrooms, within two miles. Nothing in the area sells for less than $50,000.

I went online to Realtor.com. Two interesting listings but I need a local realtor to represent me. I meet with an experienced realtor in town who I have known for years and who also owns rental properties.

Property #1:

400 yards from Concord. Walk to campus in a few minutes. Foreclosure with EVERYTHING gone. Essentially a shell. Fourth bedroom is in a converted basement, but the fifth I would have to build out underneath the 2nd floor back deck. Too expensive. Has a double garage, add $200 mo. Parking for 5-6 cars. This close to campus, say $400 per bedroom, times five, $2000 plus $200 (garage) equals $2,200 per month. Taxes are a low $200 per month. Price: $119,000. Rehab: $70,000+. At a purchase price of $80,000 the numbers work. I offer $70,000. Declined with no counter. Days on Market (DOM) 60. I'm too early. Four months pass, two price reductions, sold for $80,000! But not to me!

Property #2:

Joey, my son and fellow investor, is with me as we visit a two-bedroom (surprising 1,250 sq feet), one bath for $100,000, 1.2 miles from campus. DOM 145. A bank will usually drop the price after 60-90 DOM.

The property has major drawbacks for a family buyer.

1. Front door is DIRECTLY on a two-lane, well-traveled road. No sidewalk or curb.
2. Three feet to the left is a well-attended blue-collar, biker type bar.
3. Two bedrooms. Only 15% of buyers want a 2 bedroom house.

The buyer will be an investor with a plan.

Now the good stuff.

1. A huge 20' by 30' side deck overlooking a wooded hill flowing down to the picturesque Chester Creek. Joey and I are on the deck, admiring the view, he turns to me, "This deck is a party waiting to happen. Guys would love it. This will rent."

2. 1.2 miles from Concord.

3. Parking: An innovative expansion would do four spaces, with unlimited parking 50 yards down the road. Guys would walk.

I put on my bedroom-finder-cap to solve the two-bedrooms one-bath problem. Second floor has two bedrooms, one full bathroom. One bedroom was a large 15' x 21'. A hallway (36") halfway down the left side could split the room into two decent sized bedrooms. Home Depot wall closets to save space. *Three*, getting warmed up. The 1st floor has a living room (front of house, exit door to street) adjacent to a dining room, kitchen in the rear. Close off the exit door to the street, put up a wall and door, closing off two-thirds of living room—big bedroom—Zappo! Number *four*! The expanded dining room is now a large TV social room.

The basement's 100 years old but goes the full 40' length of the house. Let's redesign it into living space. I picture a mechanical room, left front of basement, to include a new propane (natural gas not on the street) furnace replacing the oil furnace, gas hot water heater, well pump (I'm keeping the well as public water is not available) pressure cylinder, sewer pit and pump. Next to it will be a full bathroom, toilet, vanity, stand up shower, apartment-type stacked washer/dryer. Two good-sized bedrooms separated by the stairs. *Six* bedrooms! I can't resist adding two glass sliders and 6' by 8' decks (see picture) overlooking the woods and stream! Sex sells!

Original asking price $119,000, DOM 60 reduced to $100,000, DOM 145 down to $80,000. No offers have been made. I figure the bank is desperate. I do a Zillow.com (Try it. Estimates RE values in seconds.) Comes in $181,000 After renovations, six bedrooms, two full baths, should be worth more than $181,000.

I fill out a Pre-Offer Property Worksheet. Rehab totaled $90,000 including a mandatory Government Mafia sewer tie-in of $11,500 plus $6,000 for plumber totals $17,500. Most Investors or a family won't consider a two-bedroom one bath with a $17,500 tie in, directly on a road, next to a bar. Joe, make a really ridiculous offer. OK, $40,000. Cash, no inspections and a 45-day settlement. I include the well company's estimate of $3,450 to replace the frozen well pump and mechanical jets. Bank comes back at $60,000. I feel strong. They have to get rid of it. I countered $42,500. Taxes $200 a month, insurance $50. Back at the house with Joey, it is Fall, we are on the deck looking down at a kaleidoscope of colors, Chester Creek flowing, Joey again echoed the magic words "This will rent."

The bank countered at $47,500. The realtor said that in his 30 years it was the lowest price he had seen in the town. I accepted.

By The Numbers

PURCHASE PRICE	SETTLEMENT COSTS	REHAB	RENT	PITI	GROSS MARGIN	EXPENSES	MONTHLY NET	ANNUAL NET
$47,500	$4,000	$90,000	$1950	$1,300	$650	$175	$475	$5700

A Net of $475 a month is good. The bank appraisal was $181,000. Same as Zillow. Maybe that's where appraisers get their values?

STUDENT RENTAL RULES

1) **SEASON:** Student Rental Rules. Students look and rent during the Spring and Summer to move in about 1 August. The timing of your marketing should be the same.

2) **MARKETING:**

   a. CraigsList and Facebook. First place kids look.

   b. One page flyer with pictures posted on campus on bulletin boards with phone number pull off tabs.

   c. Flyer goes to your current student rentals with a $250 commission if they refer a group that rents from you.

   d. Visit the University Housing Director with the flyer and pictures of your property.

   e. Visit athletic teams, clubs, organizations, their coaches and captains, these students already are bonded and presumably would like to live together.

   f. Local newspapers: ad with specific information directed at students such as – ½ mile from Concord University.

3) **STUDENT RENTAL APPLICATION:** Students, for the most part, don't have substantial income or a credit history score. Their parents generally pay the rent. My student application is a simple one page form asking their basic information and their parents information. I do not generally credit check the student or parents. I will perform a Home Visit if they are coming from a private house and will speak with the current or past Landlord. I also judge them by their appearance, manners and deportment.

4) **PARENTS MEETING:** Before signing the lease I hold a meeting at the house, let the students "show off" the house to their parents and answer mostly parent questions. Some parents are very protective and ask pointed questions. I stay positive, smile and answer matter of fact. I go over the main parts of the lease. I remain in control. It is my house, my lease. The kids have already decided on the house. I don't alter the lease. "My attorney won't let me". If all is positive I have the students sign the lease at this

meeting. I don't ask the parents to sign, though some student landlords have parents sign. I may, in the future, have at least one parent, with real estate in my State of Pennsylvania, sign. If some parents want to "think it over" or show their attorney the lease, fine. I let them know other groups are looking to rent the house.

5) **STRICT LEASE:** The town and neighbors are not happy with the expanding University student population especially if students live on their block. Therefore, out of necessity, my lease is tough. It does not allow parties, limits the number of people in the house and on the grounds at one time, limits number of cars parked at the property and does not allow anyone under 21 drinking alcohol in the house or grounds.

I find the key elements of control is the students' fear of a) University sanctions b) Derogatory impact on their credit bureau rating c) Police Incident Reports or arrests for noise or underage drinking d) Late charges e) Not having their lease renewed f) Parents anger. I use all the above as needed.

6) **STUDENT POTTY TRAINING:** This may be their first "out of home" or "out of college dormitory" living experience. A little like potty training. I place a sign on the refrigerator with garbage days, recycle days, time garbage is to be out and back. I have them all walk, with an empty can, to where it is placed for pickup and walk back. I have them set the thermostat. Show them the sewer pipe cleanout. Go over the dos and don'ts of parking. What is and what is not to be left out on the porch or deck. Lawn, grass, snow. Then, if problems arise, I immediately mail them a Violation of the Lease form. If serious problems arise, I hold a meeting at their house and spell out the problem and solution. Once they know the rules and are trained, in general, it goes smoothly.

7) **ONGOING RELATIONSHIP:** I or my manager attempt to have a positive, friendly ongoing relationship with the students. Why? We want them to stay, have them replace graduating students with new tenants and refer us to other groups. An ongoing relationship makes sense for both parties.

ANOTHER EXAMPLE OF A STUDENT HOUSE WE OWN

Student Housing books I recommend are:

- <u>University Wealth</u> by Marleen Geyen. Short but very good. Contains the expense % of rent rule and the Cash on Cash%. She is a smart lady.

- <u>Profit by Investing in Student Housing</u> by Michael H. Zaransky. High powered Investor discovers Student Housing.

Chapter Eleven

Making Ridiculous Offers

And Sometimes Getting Ridiculous Buys

".... then make a ridiculous offer. That's right! The word is **Ri-di-cu-lous**." Stunned silence.

"That's what I said and that's what I mean. **Ri-di-cu-lous**." He turned and wrote RIDICULOUS in big letters on the easel. The seminar leader, Bob, a PhD in Business Administration, turned and good naturedly smiled at our confusion.

"But why would you....." Bob held up his hand.

"You've spent the day looking at ten houses, three fit your requirements. Except for the price. Make three written ridiculous offers. Offers so low that you actually feel embarrassed making them, at least for the first few times you do it." He smiled broadly.

"What would the real estate agent do?"

"Your Agent works for you. She is legally obligated to present any written offers to the seller or his agent. She must present the offers. MUST."

"But what if she...."

"Make offers in writing. A small down payment check and a 24 or 48 hour time of acceptance. Bolsters your credibility. Hand, email or fax them to your Agent. Remember you don't have to justify anything! Absolutely nothing! The seller has an asking price. ASKING. I repeat ASKING. You are responding with an OFFER. It's not an insult, it's an OFFER. Don't emotionalize it."

"What's the logic behind it?"

"First, you generally have little if any information[12] on the Seller or bank's current motivation and financial condition. The Seller (Bank) may be desperate. There's one way to find out. Make a ridiculous offer. Second, you are FRAMING the parameters of the negotiation.

---

[12] Exception is how many Days on Market (DOM) the house has been , PMP and any price reductions.

You are defining the characters, dialogue, lighting and props of the play. Your opponent will react to your offer."

"How do Sellers (banks) respond to such a dramatic difference in price?"

"Three ways: (1) rejection in various forms, such as silence (2) a counter offer based on your offer's parameters (3) acceptance."

"Sometimes they accept it?"

"Sometimes. Not often. But most importantly you are testing the bottom and FRAMING the negotiation. Like a camera FRAMES a picture."

"What about the offer's contingencies?"

"Depends on your cash position, financing availability and what you really want. With cash offers, you may present no contingencies or as few as possible. No inspections, quick settlement, $1,000 down another $2,000 upon them signing. If you need owner financing for the 1st or 2nd mortgage include that but with a low rate, 30 year amortization, no balloon, assumable, and perhaps an early payoff discount. Ask for the sky. We're dealing in fantasy. You are the author."

"And Investors have been successful with this approach?"

"Very successful. You don't know what the Seller wants or will agree to until you ask. Sometimes factors like seller financing, settlement date, furniture in the property, anything really, can take precedence over price. So you ask for it all, then grudgingly and slowly give up what the seller wants to get what you want. Make sure as you give up anything you also take something. But the Seller might be desperate and accept the offer outright. You don't know until you ask."

"And you entertain counter offers?"

"Of course. This is a negotiation. But first test the bottom with a ridiculous offer in serious wrappings. No verbal offers. They carry no weight. Do it in writing. You may get back a counter offer reflecting your starting point, not theirs."

Bob acknowledged a student raising her hand. "We're spending time on low offers but with financing amortized over 20 years does a low price really matter?"

"Excellent question. I'm glad you asked", Bob said as he went behind the podium, picked up a large sign and held it above his head as he walked around the room, like those skimpily dressed girls do between rounds at a boxing match. The sign read, "YOU MAKE YOUR MONEY WHEN YOU BUY!"

"Let's all say it loudly," Bob said. "YOU MAKE YOUR MONEY WHEN YOU BUY!" we complied weakly. "Try that again, YOU MAKE YOUR MONEY WHEN YOU BUY!" It was louder, but still slightly embarrassed.

Bob laughed, put down the sign and picked up a stack of papers on the podium.

"I'm going to hand out a few examples as to why buying right is central, and I do mean central, to making money in real estate."

YOU MAKE YOUR MONEY WHEN YOU BUY

		Purchase					Mo
		Price	Rent	- PITI	- GM	- Expenses =	Net
1)	John	80,000	1,250	800	450	212	238
2)	Sam	70,000	1,250	720	530	212	318 (33% more #1)
3)	Jennie	60,000	1,250	640	610	212	398 (67% more #1)
4)	Theresa	50,000	1,250	560	690	212	478 (100% more #1)

"Let's go over this", said Bob. "$1,000 borrowed at 7% amortized over 20 years costs $8 a month; $10,000 borrowed costs $80; $20,000 costs $160 month; $30,000 costs $240 month. Jennie (#3) buys for $20,000 less than John (#1) and saves $160 a month and Nets 67% more. Theresa (#4) buys $30,000 less than John (#1) and saves $240 a month and Nets 100% more."

"Can you see how vital it is to buy low?" Bob said.

Eyes glazed. Mouths open. Heads nod.

RIDICULOUS OFFERS, BUYS AND DEALS DONE

"The next page has examples of actual deals done. I will read it aloud and you follow along. Questions at the end of each deal.", Bob said.

1) "Stand alone house, REO[13], major rehab, needed sewer hook-up costing $15,000 plus plumber's labor and material cost of $6,000 or $21,000 total, original asking price of $140,000, Zillow at $240,000[14], good area, reduced to $100,000 with DOM 120, I offered $40,000. Bank counters at $60,000. They were reacting to the ridiculous offer! I moved

---

[13] Real Estate Owned, generally by a bank

[14] Zillow.com gives an estimate of value based on sales on the block and neighborhood but is not accurate as to a specific house since it does not know its condition.

to $42,000. Always go up slowly in small increments." Bob looked at us, waiting for it to sink in.

"Remember, You make your money when you buy. Don't spend 20 years paying off a buying mistake. Bank came back at $50,000. I did a last and final offer of $45,000, which they accepted."

2) "Row house, MLS on Realtor.com with an Individual seller, needed minor rehab, asking $69,900, Zillow.com reports it's worth $76,00; offered $40,000, Seller countered $64,900, I wouldn't counter, 60 days later DOM 150, Seller reduced price to $55,000. I offered $42,000. They accepted."

3) "Row house, REO, major rehab but has 1.5 bathrooms, reduced from $85,000 to $59,900 to $48,000, DOM 317, Zillow is $78,000, offered $40,000, Bank's agent said two other Investor offers, best and last, I offered $44,100, they accepted. The $100 was in case another Investor offered $44,000".

4) "Stand alone, REO Short Sale, minor rehab, originally asking $90,000, Zillow says $110,000, I offer $50,000, no counter, 45 days pass, bank drops asking price to $50,000, I don't just accept their 50,000 but offer a ridiculous 40,000. They accept."

5) "Very interesting stand alone in resort area, MLS on Realtor.com, Individual seller, major rehab, original asking price $100,000, Zillow reports $215,000, DOM 192, drops to $70,000, widow living there wants out, I offer $55,000, $1,000 down, contingent on a Bank's 1st mortgage with widow holding a 2nd mortgage for the remaining balance at 5% amortized over 25 years. Widow counters at $70,000, will hold the 2nd mortgage but at 8%, 5 yr balloon. Using only $1000 of my own money is central to me, so I accept her price and interest rate but counter with the balloon at 10 years. Widow accepts because price was central to her."

6) "Twin, REO, original asking price $88,000, Zillow reports $132,000, major rehab, could be a flip or a rental, DOM 120, reduced to $55,000, I offer $32,500, Bank counters at $40,000, I counter at $35,000, they accept."

"Are there any questions" Bob asks.

"But ridiculous isn't applicable in all offers?"

"True, it is only one weapon in your arsenal and it is not useful in all situations. Occasionally, with an REO, the original asking price may be ridiculously low or a sudden drop may be ridiculous. The bank may need to be out quickly. Estate sales can be fertile ground. If you see a super bargain jump on it with both feet. Depending on circumstances you may even offer above the asking price. Fight to snare a super bargain."

"How do you handle the rejection?"

"Don't take it personally. If you make a lot of offers, you receive a lot of rejections. It's the way the game is played. "

"My agent really discourages me, actually won't allow me to make really low offers. He says it's a waste of his - "

Bob's hand shoots up.

"Let's talk about your agent. He gets paid by making a sale, any sale, bargain or not. His short-term earnings are not in line with your best interests. His long-term interests are in line if you are successful and continue to buy. But maybe he's embarrassed, maybe he's lazy, maybe he just doesn't understand. You sit him down and educate him as to what you are doing, why you are doing it and his role. If he doesn't become a positive member of your team, replace him."

"So you make lots of offers?"

"It's a numbers game. The more ridiculous offers, the more possibility one will be accepted. But be careful to only make offers on properties you have a completed Pre-Offer Property Worksheet, you want to own, and can finance."

SYNOPSIS OF BOB'S SEMINAR ON NEGOTIATION

NEGOTIATING 101. 1) Start with a ridiculously low offer, include in as many advantageous contingencies with an individual seller. 2) If a cash offer, especially for an REO, have no contingencies. 3) Go up slowly in small increments. 4) Give up areas that are important to the seller to get what is important to you. 5) Don't take rejection personally. 6) Put houses you like on the "Watch List" at Realtor.com, even after a rejected offer. If not sold within 30 or 60 days, banks or other sellers will reduce the price.

REHABS AS BARGAINS! Today the bargains are those properties that need a rehab. Most are REOs. The worse the condition, the lower the price. The family buyer doesn't want a rehab and can't finance it. FHA, Fannie Mae and Freddie Mac won't finance a house needing a rehab. This leaves investors. The very best bargains need a rehab AND a creative solution to whatever problem the property has. Many investors are poor at creative solutions in space utilization, design and which amenities to choose. If you don't have this talent perhaps your GC, family member, employee or interior designer may help. Try the team approach.

NEGATIVE MONTHLY NET–NEVER, EVER! The higher your offer price, the higher your mortgage amount, the higher your monthly payment. This will reduce your GM and Net. Some investors foolishly finance themselves into a negative monthly Net. They rationalize that the other benefits of real estate investing (depreciation, appreciation, principal paid down, business expenses, etc.) offset the negative monthly Net. Not so. Quite stupid actually. Do not do this. The most important number is your positive monthly Net. The other benefits will always be there IF YOU HAVE A POSITIVE NET which enables you to make the monthly mortgage payments, manage and maintain the property.

LET'S TAKE A LOOK AT VARIOUS FINANCING SCENARIOS

1. 100% FINANCING GIVES YOU CASH ON CASH% AT INFINITY!

Purchase	Settlement	Rehab	Total Costs	Permanent Financing Mortgage	Cash Out	PITI	Rent	Gross Margin	Adm/ Maint/ 17%	Monthly Net	Annual Cash In	Cash on Cash %
$40K	$5K	$25K	$70K	$70K	0	$800	$1300	$450	$221	$229	$2,748	Infinite

How it was done. Original asking price $100,000, asking price at time of offer $79,900. First Ridiculous Offer was $35,000. REO. They countered at $45,000. My final offer was $40,000, which they accepted. Purchase price, settlement cost and rehab paid cash from an IRA. Commercial bank appraises at $100,000 after rehab, lends 70%, at 7%, 20 yr. amortization, 5 yr. balloon. Section 8 tenant, 4 bed, 1.5 ba. at 1300 mo.

2. HOME EQUITY LINES OR 2ND MORTGAGES CAN CREATE CLOSE TO 100% LEVERAGE

Purchase	Settlement	Rehab	Total	Mortgage 1st and 2nd	Cash Out	PITI w/ 1st & 2nd Mortgage	Rent	Gross Margin	Adm/ Maint/ 17%	Monthly Net	Annual Cash In	Cash on Cash %
$64K	$5K	$28K	$97K	$65K $31K $96K	$1,000	$940	$1275	$335	$217	$118	$1,416	172%

How it was done. Original asking price $109,900. REO, asking price at time of our offer $88,000. 1st Ridiculous Offer $50,000, We negotiated to $64,000. Primary mortgage $65,000,

30 yr. 5.5% FHA primary home owner loan, Principal and Interest of 1st primary mortgage at $320 mo, Home Equity Loan $31,000 (house appraised at $135,000 after rehab) at 4.5% over 10 yrs. This does not meet our Gross Margin and Net *standard* but a Cash on Cash of 172% is excellent.

Negotiating is FUN. It's a chase. Snagging a prize. The following are good cheap reference books. Try Amazon.

- Give and Take by Chester Karrass. Karrass has other books and courses. Excellent.
- Getting to Yes, by Roger Fisher and William Ury. An interesting perspective. Very good and different.
- You Can Negotiate Anything, Herb Cohen. Excellent, the basics.

Chapter Twelve

How I Found the Houses

20% of your time produces 80% of your Results

This is an easy chapter. It's not hard to find good buys today (2012) if you know what you're looking for in the areas you have chosen.

Let's assume you are following my niche of 4/5 bedroom houses in good school districts. You might think by the previous sentence that you and your real estate agents would search, visit and make offers to acquire only 4/5 bedroom houses, right? No.

Most of the houses I buy have 3 bedrooms. I find or create the other bedrooms. I do buy 4 and very occasionally a 5 bedroom. But when I buy a 4 bedroom I am looking for possibilities for creating a 5th bedroom.

TEACHING POINT: The more (legitimate by code) bedrooms you have, the higher the rent, Gross Margin and Net.

In Chapter Seven, I explained what the criteria of a bedroom is – but let's go over that again: (a) 70 sq ft with neither the width or length less than 7 ft, (b) Ceiling must be 7 ft, (c) Must have direct egress to door or window. If the egress is to a window, it must be 5.7 sq ft and start no higher than 44" from the floor. (d) Heat. That's it.

What I look for in a house

1. Row or Twins – Have our Pre-Offer Property Worksheet A with you.

    A. Can I finish the basement and put in additional bedrooms? Look at ceiling height and egress. Heat can be fluid-filled electric baseboard heaters. Be aware of water problems – if there are problems, a French drain and one or two sump pumps may be necessary.

    B. Front or rear porch? Does it qualify as a bedroom? 70 sq. ft. with width and length each 7 ft.? I take out all but one front window on a multiple windowed front porch.

C. In a large living room, could a bedroom be built? Remember it must have a window and heat.

D. Does it have 1.5 or 2 full bathrooms? A four bedroom tenant may have 5/6 people. One bathroom is a problem. I put powder rooms or, under unusual circumstances, a full bathroom in during initial rehab. I need two bathrooms to hold the tenant there.

E. Do windows need to be replaced? Are hardwood floors under the carpet? Most houses built 70+ years ago have hardwood floors under the carpet.

F. Electrical panel old? Fuses? Knob and tube wiring? How many lines from box into house? A row or twin should have a minimum of ten lines. Washer and dryer hook-up? We standardize on electric dryers. We totally rewire many of our rehabs and have 15 or more lines into the panel box. We install a 30-slot panel from Home Depot.

G. Plumbing – Ancient? Corrugated lines? Where is the cleanout? Is the sewer/soil line in good shape? Are copper lines old and turning blue/green? Sink/shower faucets/traps/diverter in good shape?

H. HVAC – furnace/boiler – old? I replace oil with natural gas. If gas is not in the house, not on the street (not available from the utility company), I bring in propane. If it has central air, I take it out. They can buy window AC units.

I. Roof – How old? Shingles or flat? Gutters, downspouts, siding in good shape?

2. Single detached

A. How many square feet? 1,500 sq ft and above is a good sized house, and therefore, potential bedrooms may appear upon inspection.

B. Basement, does it have egress? Does it have a walkout door? Ceiling height 7 ft.? Remember it's easy to add heat in a basement and basements stay cool in the summer.

C. Front and rear porch, convert to bedroom? What are the width and length dimensions?

D. Does it already have a powder room or 1/2 bath?

Experience is the great teacher. Go out and look at 100 houses and you'll become a bedroom finder. Fill out 100 Pre-Offer Property Worksheets.

How I Buy Houses

1. **Buying properties with a Real Estate Agent (representing me) and using the Multiple Listing Service (MLS.)** When I say MLS, I mean as found on Realtor.com or a commercial real estate company's website. This is the normal way most people buy houses. Overall for **76% of our purchased houses we used a real estate agent and the house was listed in the MLS.** The first few years I spent 80% of my prospecting time on the following 2 through 5 methods of acquiring houses. Now I spend 95% of my limited prospecting time using Realtor.com (the MLS) on line with two knowledgeable, experienced, investor-friendly real estate agents. In 2008, 2009, 2010 and 2011 **85%** of my houses were purchased with a real estate agent with houses on the MLS. It's simple, direct, computerized. This is where you spend your time.

2. **Buying properties directly from Individuals, without a Real Estate Agent.**
   Overall 18%) were purchased directly from individuals such as other investors, For Sale by Owners, friends of friends etc. They, without effort, fall into your lap.

3. **Sheriff Sale**
   1 house (2%) from a Sheriff Sale. Waste of time.

4. **Judicial Tax Sale**
   1 house (2%) from a Judicial Tax Sale. Waste of time unless you are an experienced and knowledgeable investor, have been inside the house and know the owner won't contest the sale, which in this case I did.

5. **Subject to Sale**
   1 house (2%) from a Subject to Sale. Problem is lack of financing for settlement costs, rehab costs, etc. Waste of time.

CONCLUSIONS: As long as the foreclosure/REO cloudburst continues, use real estate agents and the MLS to find bank owned REOs. REO houses are priced low but generally need a rehab. A house needing a significant amount of work eliminates family buyers and Fannie Mae/Freddie Mac/FHA financing. Leaves you and other investors. Today fifty percent or more of investors cannot get financing. Find the REO houses that fit your niches and make offers. If the price is already a bargain, get in and fight for the good ones.

Let's go over all your options. I've studied and tried every option below so don't waste your time on those that take marketing, (I tried signs, mailings, flyers - don't bother unless you are a masochist) substantial time and require intricate knowledge. We'll start with the worst and work our way out of the mud into the sunshine.

1. **Short Sales** - I've read the books, bought a course and tried and tried. Very slow process. Very frustrating. You have no control. With such a long (3-6 months or more) process there's plenty of time for something bad to happen, and it does. I was never successful. Wasted a lot of time. If you truly hate someone tell them short sales are the ticket to an easy fortune. Caveat: However, if the short sale is on the MLS, this is different and I have bought several this way. But you may have to wait months for an answer.

2. **Sheriff Sales** — A complicated, sophisticated process. You really have to be an experienced investor. You never get inside the property before you buy it. Any liens on the property stay with the property and must be paid by you the buyer. Wonderful isn't it? No financing. 10% cash down at Sheriff's Sale and the rest in cash in 10 days. I spent a lot of time reading, researching, going to sheriff sales, making offers and finally bought one property (#27). Cheap but a run-out-in-the-street-and-throw-up mess. Dead dog on the property. Odor. I still smell it.

Today (2012) Sheriff Sales are worse than ever. Banks are unloading their houses into the Sheriff Sale with a high set price no one will pay. The bank then retains it, gives it to an REO realtor who puts it into the MLS at a reasonable price. Forget the Sheriff Sale and concentrate on the REOs as they resurface in the MLS.

3. **Subject To Sales** – Many books, seminars and courses tout this method of obtaining the deed while leaving the seller's mortgage in place. I purchased the books, bought a course, obtained the forms and learned the process and whoopee! I finally did one (#35) with an MLS individual sale. But I paid all settlement costs (the seller is usually broke) both brokers' commission, the rehab and paid PITI for 4 months before a renter moved in. No way to finance all these costs and therefore my CASH ON CASH% is far below the 25% standard. Not a good deal. Today it cash flows and is an OK investment. After

26 years (mortgage paid off) it will be a great investment but you and I want great investments NOW!

4. **Individual Sales** - Defined as sales between individuals without a real estate agent or the MLS. They happen by themselves. You are out in the marketplace looking at properties, talking with real estate agents, lawyers, bankers, investors and sellers. You belong to real estate investment groups and attend their meetings. You continuously hand out cards, talk with small groups in the hallway, over lunch, at the bar. You are making offers, rehabbing, renting and you meet people and good things happen. Get people's cards, their name, phone number, make friends. Talk to everyone.

EXAMPLES OF INDIVIDUAL SALES

A real estate agent sells me a house through the MLS. After settlement he says, "I own a property you may like." Empty. Low price. I buy. Offers me another. Empty. Beat up. Very low price. I buy. He was choking on both.

I'm rehabbing on a street I like. There's a dumpster down a few houses. I walk over. Investor/rehabber shows me through. Says "I didn't think it was this bad." I nod. "You like it?" he says. I nod. "Make me an offer." I do. He nods.

Someone tells someone. For sale by owner. I hand out my card. You never know. It takes no time because there is no plan except to keep your eyes open to possible opportunities.

5. **Judicial Tax Sale** – This is the second stage of the tax sale process. You don't get inside the property before buying. Only for the sophisticated investor. You buy without liens, but title insurance sometimes is difficult to get. Helps to have inside information and know the area very well.

6. **Real Estate Agent/Multiple Listing Service** – This method is by far the easiest. I spend time prospecting on Realtor.com or another commercial website using the MLS on line. I have a Watch List and get computerized updates to my searches. I also receive daily computerized listing updates from my agents. The whole thing takes little time and thus is the most effective. 86% of my purchases from 2008 to present were from this method. All real estate agents and companies put their listings in the MLS, which everyone, including you, have access to 24/7. Log on to Realtor.com, or a commercial site, put in

your parameters and let it rip. Build up a Watch List. DOM (Days On Market) increases, price drops, you scoop down from the sky like an eagle. ZAP!

Have favored real estate agents who live and work in different geographical areas, school districts, or municipalities you are interested in. The agents will, using your parameters, program their company's computer to automatically run MLS searches every day and email the results to you. Agents want to sell houses and make money. Educate them as to EXACTLY what you are looking for. Be specific. Visit houses with them. Point out what you like and don't like. Write it up. Email, fax or hand it out. You provide her kid's education, family vacations, funds for her IRA. She works for you. Work with her.

I have two main agents. You don't want too many competing against one another. If you find an MLS property and it's in her "area", let her represent you. Loyalty begets loyalty. One of my agents, knowing exactly what I want, visits interesting properties for me and emails me the results. The other provides short-term financing.

Today there are a lot of smiling Chest Hairs on the web touting internet real estate riches. But today it's bank REOs on Realtor.com with a few agents in different areas. Simple, efficient, web friendly and productive.

TEACHING POINT: Bargains. Very low priced bank-owned REOs, newly placed on the MLS, are sold in days, and sometimes even hours. Or a bank, with a DOM of 60, suddenly drops the price $20,000. ZAP! For these you offer quickly. Sometimes at full price. Sometimes over. Fight for a good bargain!

Chapter Thirteen

Referrals: Assembling Your Team

How Did You Meet Your Spouse?

In our computerized Facebook/Twitter information-overloaded age the ancient tradition of people to people, word of mouth, the grapevine, still prevail on all important matters.

How did your sister meet her husband? How did your sick uncle meet his surgeon? How did your mother meet your father? How did you decide on a school district for your kids?

People generally don't meet their spouses in singles bars. Some may spend considerable time, energy and money somewhere between the bar stools and have a few congratulatory sleepovers as compensation. But people meet their spouses informally. Friend of a friend, friend to lover, neighbor, work, wedding, party, school, vacation or Mom arranges.

People live, associate and do business with those like themselves. Scientific fact.

Intelligence, schooling, vocation, hobbies, values, social standing, religion/God, physical attractiveness, the list goes on. You have "something in common." The more in common the better chance the marriage or relationship of any kind has to last.

If a friend's mother develops cancer do they flip through the yellow pages or Google oncologists? Of course not! They trust the older than dirt people-to-people network and ask around. They call people they trust, who lead them to more people and then to doctors, appointments, doctor-to-doctor referrals, appointments, BINGO! Health is too important to be left to the cold self-serving advertisements of strangers. We want a referral from someone we trust who had the same need. If they are happy, we should be also.

Competent successful business people surround themselves with folks made of the same stuff. To surround yourself with a team of competent contractors, specialists, agents, a lawyer and CPA, first talk with other successful real estate investors. Search them out. Introduce yourself to ones you admire. Join and attend the local real estate investor group meetings. Ask about the always-elusive prey, good contractors. Write down the names, phone numbers, what they do, cheap/expensive, how long using them, etc. Call the referrals, meet with them, tell them what you need. Be forthright; have them fill out an application. You will get an impression, a feel for them. Ask for and call their recent references. Do your homework up front. Try out the ones that make sense. If the contractors are good, try to establish a relationship. No one is perfect, including you and me. Divorce is expensive. Some need a short leash. Others can handle a longer one. Manage them. Pay them on the spot when a job is done. (I carry checks with me.) Sometimes the devil you know is better than the devil you don't know. But keep looking. It's an ongoing process.

Below are my current team members (all through referrals)

I.   Professional/White Collar
     1.) CPA with real estate expertise. He invests in rental houses, competent.
     2.) Attorney with RE expertise. Business attorney, smart, concerned.
     3.) Insurance agent with RE investor expertise. Deals with other RE investors.
     4.) Two real estate brokers who have experience with investors.
     5.) Four banks or mortgage brokers.
     6.) Title company

I found these workers through referrals, and by stopping in to local businesses with good reputation, a referral of sorts. 100% referrals if we include the stop-ins.

II.   Contractors/Specialists, my current team

     1.) Two general contractors
     2.) Two handymen
     3.) Roofer
     4.) Ceramic tile setter
     5.) Hardwood refinisher
     6.) Master plumber and plumber apprentice
     7.) One licensed and one unlicensed electrician
     8.) Two HVAC
     9.) Sewer service (Roto Rooter type)
     10.) Dumpster company
     11.) Kitchen cabinets and countertop
     12.) Concrete company

Of these, I found 55% through referrals, and the other 45% I found through Craigslist ads. However the 9 Craigslist contractors, have been my high turnover, shoddy work, Iwantmoneynow problems.

I have not been able to obtain competent and inexpensive general contractor referrals and, therefore, GCs have been a particularly expensive problem. Roofers are not far behind. Handymen less so but not good. Where I have not received good referrals (GC, roofer, handymen, ceramic tile setter) I have put forth time and money and been rewarded with pain. Yet

by running the Craigslist gauntlet of Contractors from Hell! I currently have two competent GCs, one roofer, two competent handymen and a ceramic tile setter. I have no answer to finding cheap/quality GCs, roofers, handymen, ceramic tile setters without investing the time consuming blind man's bluff Craigslist Contractor Day game in full body armor.

III.   Administrative: Try referrals, but Craigslist for administrative help works well

    1.)Bookkeeper P/T 2 nights /and Saturdays
    2.) Asst Manager P/T 25 hours week
    3.) Gofer - student - 15 hrs/wk

On Craigslist, I run a very specific ad of what I want, what the duties are, pay, hours, live within 10 miles, cell phone number, email me a resume/letter, I call those that look good, make an appointment, they fill out a 2 page application, interview, go over a job description with them, check referrals, run a credit, eviction and criminal check, 90 day trial! If they don't work out, I do it again.

SUMMATION

Referrals are the number one way to meet competent professionals and specialists.

Craigslist seems to be best for administrative help, GCs, roofers, handymen and ceramic tile setters. In my experience, Craigslist produces a better class of applicant than the newspaper. In writing an ad, I describe in great detail and some humor exactly what I'm looking for. They respond by email with their information and cell number. I may email back and forth, as one can tell a lot by their responses. GC's, roofers, handymen, ceramic tile setters do not have resumes.

TEACHING POINT: Spend time evaluating and researching your people before you hire. I know you're in a hurry and you need someone now. You're under the gun. Impatient. He seems OK. Says he can do it: WAIT. TAKE 3 BREATHS. DON'T PULL THE TRIGGER

Spend time upfront doing your homework. Call referrals. No referrals or no good referrals - NO. Little or no experience - NO. Negative attitude - NO. Some contractors will show pictures of their previous work, which can be helpful, but if their pictures are not great, then see what their other work looks like. Run a credit, eviction and criminal check. Do your homework upfront. Because you will spend 20 times and thousands, perhaps 10's of thousands of dollars, if you contract with the wrong contractor or professional or administrator. The wrong person is very expensive, time consuming (firing someone ruins your week!) and outright debilitating. I know.

Believe me. I know.

Chapter Fourteen

Contractors from Hell!

How To Meet, Evaluate, And Attempt To Control Contractors

Let's you and I have a heart to heart. You know by now my learning experiences have been painful and costly. I hope you learn from my errors and follow the guidelines in this very important chapter.

My most persistent problems have been with general contractors (GCs). Not tenant management, not finding, not financing and not purchasing properties. Hands down GCs win. Roofers second. Third place a tie between handymen and ceramic tile pretenders. Next in line are the specialists, who earn their licenses by taking courses, passing a professionally sanctioned test and/or serving an apprenticeship i.e., Plumbers, Electricians and HVAC (Heating and Air Conditioning)

Back to the GCs. You may think that general contractors are in business to practice their trade. Not so. They are in the business of extracting money from investors and homeowners. They are skilled, innovative, successful and highly motivated. Let your guard down for two seconds, be empathetic, be FAIR, help them out (The social worker in me!) and you are run over, flat on your back, money gone, watching their taillights fade. "What just happened?"

I'm not overstating the problem. Here are two reasons why.

1. ANYONE CAN BE A GENERAL CONTRACTOR!

You could! Your unemployed uncle could! Anyone! No classes to attend, tests to take and pass, no license to earn, no apprenticeship to journey through, no capital or credit requirements, don't need a driver's license, truck, tools or machines. All you have to say is, "I am a general contractor" three times, click your heels and Presto! That's it. You got it! YOU ARE A GENERAL CONTRACTOR! Only in America, baby!

2. GC's and specialists are price tiered by the market according to their skills and ability to deliver great, good, average or poor work. Like all businesses, the good ones who produce a consistently superior product, work hard, meet deadlines, have capital, are going upscale to make

the big bucks. The good ones want to deal with homeowners improving a $500,000 plus house, rehab a room for a bank or put an addition on a school or government building. Higher end clients demand quality and are willing to pay for it. God bless them. But that ain't rental houses.

Rehabbing and maintaining rental houses is lower priced work. What I call Wholesale. High-end GC's and specialists charge Retail which is the going rate for quality and reliability, but the rehab and maintenance of a rental house must be done CHEAPLY. (Doesn't the word sound exactly what it means?) Yet, we also must have quality. But Wholesale. A dichotomy. Two forces, foreign to each other, attempting to coexist but always the friction, you as arbitrator and referee.

Pay Retail and it will eat your Net profits alive. Can't make a profit paying retail. Therefore, because you can only pay Wholesale, you are left, conceptually, with the market's bottom tier of GC's and Specialists. Side Note: As I write this in 2012 the United States is in a prolonged real estate recession. Construction is down more than 50%. Without work, the top and middle tier contractors are gravitating down to . . . Wholesale. Good for me and you.

THINGS NOT TO DO. NEVER. EVER.

1) **DON'T let the pay get ahead of the work**. The cardinal of all sins. MONEY IS YOUR ONLY REAL LEVERAGE. This is a matter of Power and Control. It's you or him giving orders. Stay way behind (20-30%) in paying and hold on to a substantial amount (10% or more) till 100% of the last punch list item is completed and inspected by you and the municipality's inspector, for if the municipality's building inspector doesn't pass the work, the house cannot be rented.

2) **DON'T pay time and materials**. A license to steal. GCs sell it. They love it—an hourly rate, a day rate. NO. If they can't estimate a job, it's their problem. Tell them, "You are the contractor, give me a price."

3) **DON'T hire GCs with a verbal agreement and handshake**. No application to fill out, no referrals to call, no credit, criminal or eviction check. Don't visit contractor's current or past work. Consultants say trust is the cornerstone of running a good business. That is a wonderful, feel good highway to Contractor Hell!

4) **DON'T hire your own crew with you as boss.** Pay them hourly, time cards and a clock. Buy a van, pickup truck, lots of tools and machines. (As they disappear stamp ID#s on them,

keep a good inventory. Still disappearing? Spray them red so nobody will want them. Brilliant! But that doesn't work either. I tried.) Leave the crew for days at a time with the trusted Foreman because you are so busy performing other stupendous cost saving feats. Bless me Father for I have committed all the above transgressions.

5) DON'T loan the GC your tools and machines. Or give him keys or access to your garage with such. Hell, why not give him your truck or van to use! NO!

6) DON'T front the GC Material Money—cash, check made out to him or your credit card to use. If the door is left open, they will walk through. And baby, they will do so with GUSTO!

7) DON'T empathize with the GC's personal problems, financial difficulties, parole lockups, family health issues, including deaths and hospital stays. Note: If you are a tough, ruthless, successful business SOB who knows it's a jungle and you are the lion, I congratulate you. But why are you reading this book?

8) DON'T sign his contract or worse have 2 signed contracts, his and yours. NO! You are in charge, not him. He signs <u>yours</u>. The contract is the foundation of everything to follow. The contractor signing your contract, unadulterated of changes, is a mandatory start in a very difficult journey.

THINGS YOU MUST DO, ALWAYS.

1) Referrals. Ask or email other successful investors for contractors they use. Be specific—looking for a plumber in this area, an electrician in another area. In addition to the name and phone number ask how long have they used them. What type of jobs did they do for them? Average price per job? What are their strengths? What are their weaknesses? Would they recommend them? Would they use them again? But always, always do your own screening.

2) Call two/three references of the contractor. Ask if they are friends, family or church members. Best to talk with another investor as a reference. Was the job a rehab like yours or did he paint a room? How long ago? Price of job $100 or $10,000? What are the good points of GC? Areas to improve? Would he recommend him? Hire him again? Was the referral enthusiastic? Lukewarm? If a GC has excuses instead of good references—what will he do to your house? NO!

3) Contractor Application. Take control! GC or specialist fills out a one-page application, but may not expect questions like 1) Do you have a current valid driver's license? (Have them show it to you. Is it expired? Out of state? If possible photocopy it) 2) Ever been arrested? 3) Are you on parole? 4) Will you submit to a drug test? 5) Have you ever been in drug or alcohol rehab? 6) Do you give permission for DHR to run a credit check, criminal check and eviction check? 95% will fill it out. I like married GCs who own their own home, have a truck/van, valid driver's license and contractor insurance. But I take the best I can get.

When they hand the application back to you, go over it with them line by line, ask questions, make notes on the application, do a thorough job. What is the GC good at? What does he like to do? Has he done full rehabs like the job you are about to do? Who are his references… investors, homeowners, friends? What was the type and price of his last three jobs? Invest the time here so you don't lose months and $10,000 or more later.

4) Visit a current or previous job. Nothing else comes close. Actually seeing his work. What you see is what you will get. This visit is similar to the Tenant Home Visit. Both are very powerful indicators of your future success or failure.

5) Pictures. In this digital age, pictures taken by camera or cell phone can be e-mailed, printed or viewed on the camera. I have had GCs, tile setters etc. show me pictures of their work. Some have pictures on their websites. All good. The more organized and sophisticated a contractor is with pictures, website, email and referrals the better indication you have he is a competent and successful contractor.

6) Run a credit check, criminal check and eviction check. Landlord web-site, $25, 10 minutes. See how bad it is. If you wouldn't rent to him, why trust him to rehab a $100,000 asset? Some checks will surprise, some disappoint.

7) Hold a Contractors (or Specialist) Day: Put a very specific ad on Craigslist, you get better quality respondents than a newspaper ad. Hold the Contractor's Day at the rehab property. Invite all. Make appointments every 30 minutes. They arrive, hand them the application. When they are finished, go over it with them line by line. Ask questions. Mark it up. Get their references, phone numbers, prices of their jobs. Was it a rehab or did he paint a room?

Next give the GC an Exhibit A Scope of Work you have made up. Walk through with those worthy of your time. (Those not worthy, walk through themselves.) Go over the Scope of Work in each room and solicit their opinions. The experienced and smart will be knowledgeable, give perceptive observations and strong opinions. From the application and walk-through, you will have a good feel for the GC. Tell them they must email, fax or call in a

Labor Only bid within 48 hours. Good GCs who charge Retail—do you no good. Get bids. No bid from a GC you like? Call and ask when you'll receive it.

The spread of the bids will astonish you. Low bids are only good if the GC is competent. If he's a dud, a thief, or a druggie the low bid will be very expensive in the long run.

8) Why Labor Only Bids? Three Reasons.

A) LOW AND MIDDLE TIER GCS DON'T HAVE CAPITAL to buy materials for a rehab. Labor Only allows them to bid. Labor Only bids are 20 times simpler to figure than Labor and Materials. Think about it. Just labor. How many MAN DAYS per job, per room, times a day rate equals a bid price. Take an experienced GC two hours or less to work up a bid. Labor Only means you'll get more bids faster. Without bids you can't start your engine.

B) BIDDING AND CONTRACTING FOR LABOR AND MATERIAL you implicitly trust the GC to take your check and buy materials for your job. But that money is gone within an hour for rent, child support, groceries, bills, wife, kids' prescriptions, you name it. He buys materials with what's left over, which is nothing. Next week he's back, his hand out, you his ATM, singing remarkably tragic ballads. They must be true; no one could make this up! GREAT: If the contractor has capital and offers a good price including labor and materials (as outlined in Specification of Material and Methods) and is willing to front his money to buy the materials, then I would consider using him.

C) WITH LABOR ONLY, YOU CAN BETTER DIRECT THE GC to follow the Specification of Material and Methods. He must pass our open book test on the Specification to prove he knows the essentials of the Specifications before being paid his first check. If you just hand the Specification to him, he will not read it, probably lose it and buy what he is used to buying.

TEACHING POINT: You also figure a bid price! Follow the previously mentioned formula. The more times you do it, the better you get. Also, determine how many calendar days from start to finish you think is reasonable. A start/finish date is part of the contract.

OK, BACK TO THE BIDDING PROCESS. Six GCs submit labor-only bid prices. (Later I negotiate a start and end date). Bids are $6,500, $10,000, $13,000, $18,000, $24,000, $33,000. It is normal to get such a spread. I estimated the Labor Only at $12,000 with 35 calendar days. The GC with the $6,500 bid had fair but small job references, no truck and "would get insurance" if he got the job. (The Contractor Application is an invaluable tool to start with. Just as the Tenant Application is.)

The $10,000 bid is two personable guys, early/mid twenties, five years with other companies and recently on their own. Say they can do everything. Only referral is a positive referral of a $2,000 concrete job. No.

The $13,000 bid is from a middle-aged GC and his son. I call and get an excellent reference from a Philadelphia investor who he worked with for seven years doing over 30 total rehabs. Dour personality, truck, tools, no driver's license (son has one), son has the contractor insurance, can start immediately. Son has neck tattoos, expanded ear lobe jewelry, cell phone that rings constantly, wife and two small children, he breathes hard, eyeballs contract when we talk money.

I eliminate the $24,000 and $33,000 bids. The $18,000 bid will not reduce his price and can't start for five weeks. I hone in on Middle-age and Son. Visit his recently completed basement rehab job. Excellent. Super ceramic work. I negotiate Middle-age GC from $13,000 to $11,000, agree on 40 calendar days.

9) Specification test to take home. I give Middle-age and Son the open book specification test to take home and complete. NO FIRST CHECK UNTIL TEST ANSWERS ARE HANDED IN AND WE DISCUSS ANY INCORRECT ONES. I didn't spend 250+ hours for GCs to ignore the Specification. It's a 25-page Rehab Bible.

10) The Contract. The word Contractor doesn't come from the Latin word squishysoft or the Greek word pleasebeatme. CONTRACTOR comes from the word CONTRACT. They expect to sign a contract. Just as the 7 part Residential Lease is the foundation for the Tenant Landlord relationship, the 7 Part Independent Contractor Service Agreement mandates the obligations and standards the contractor must meet. I meet Middle-age and Son at the job site. We walk through the house room by room reading the Scope of Work. Middle-age makes three good suggestions I immediately incorporate into the Scope of Work. We then sit down and read through, initial and sign our 7-part Independent Contractor Services Agreement that is as tight as Scrooge before the three ghosts. The whole process takes about two hours. Here are the 7 parts:

Part 1) Independent Contractor Services Agreement. If an agreement could be beautiful, this would be Miss America. Three pages full of investor-friendly paragraphs. I read aloud each paragraph. General Contractor initials seven core paragraphs then signs at the end.

Part 2) Exhibit A Scope of Work. Six page preprinted form that leads you from the outside entrance (front yard, railing, mail box etc.) through each room of the house, into the basement and to the rear yard. It's difficult to skip or forget anything. It's all there to remind you. Under each heading I handwrite, on 4 or 5 blank lines, what I want done.

Part 3) Exhibit B Specification of Material and Methods. The Specification is mandatory and invaluable. Covers what material and items the GC will use including the SKU# at Home Depot. Includes how he will do things, and in what order. And of course the almost famous The ELIMINATORS: what not to include in a rental house. I love the Specification. Goes under my pillow each night. In my will to the kids. Family and friends will throw confetti-like bits of the Specification, not flowers, over my casket.

TEACHING POINT: I have never seen a Specification of Material and Methods in any real estate "How To" book or course. I don't understand why. Any construction company agreeing to a substantial job has a Specification as part of their Contract. Any contractor building a McDonald's has one. It's part of all building trade contracts. You need one as well.

Part 4) Exhibit C Payment Schedule. Contractor is very interested in this. Write out what is to be completed for the first pay, second pay, etc. I stop in on Fridays at which time GC hands me the receipts from his Home Depot gift card, my current material payment method. The contractor has written the property street number and his name on the top of each receipt. You inspect receipts making sure that the contractor has purchased no personal items or tools and there are no telltale gaps without a receipt. Inspect the work done. If appropriate in the rehab time table, write up a punch list with carbon paper between the sheets, including items on previous punch lists, if applicable. Stay well behind on pay! If all is 100% complete on the work for a draw payment, pay the contractor with a check.

Part 5) Exhibit D Change Order Form. Changes? Always. Write changes out in detail, with price, date and signed by both parties. Eliminates surprises at the end. "But I did xyz and it's not in the Scope of Work so I get $2500 more." Sorry. No Change Order, no money.

Part 6) Exhibit E Punch List. So very practical. Gives you and GC a method of communication. On Fridays, generally as the GC approaches job completion, I use the punch list with carbon paper so I can immediately give the GC the original and retain the copy. You and the GC sign the punch list at the bottom. His signature focuses his attention that the punch list is serious business that can stop his next draw. Eliminates the "I never got it" BS excuse. I put everything in writing so there are no "misunderstandings."

Part 7) Exhibit F Responsibility For Damages. Contractors snipe and point fingers at one another. This helps.

MORE WAYS TO CONTROL THE CONTRACTOR

A) FURTHER EXPLANATION OF THE FRIDAY AFTERNOON MEETING:

Best to arrive on site, and walk the house alone without the contractors with you- no pressure- make up new punch list with carbon paper, include last week's punch list commitments if not completed. Meet with GC, walk through house again, discuss progress, next weeks' work to get done, add items to punch list, new GC commitments. As the job approaches completion, the punch list may grow to more than 30 items. Contractor will work at the punch list items during the week and be ready next Friday. He knows his draw is on the line. I hand him a copy of the latest Contract Tracking (which is mailed to him every Monday) and we discuss the pay and time left on the contract. Write up any Change Orders on the form with carbon but do not agree on a price and additional days. Get away and think about it. As our meeting comes to an end, if he has completed all the work under a draw, I write a check. If it's not, I don't. If there's no check I don't stay around for pressure or abuse. I tell the GC why he won't get a check, hand him the punch list, walk to my car and turn off my cell phone.
WHO'S IN CONTROL? THE ONLY REAL LEVER YOU HAVE IS MONEY. USE IT TO STAY IN CONTROL.

I generally stop in unannounced at least once during the week when I'm in the area, and just walk through. Are they working hard? Or hardly working? Are they making surprising progress or just putting in time and going nowhere? Is the GC on the job hammer in hand or on someone else's job site and has subs doing the job? He'd better be on my job. Sweating. All the above is pertinent to specialists as well.

B) CONTRACT TRACKING: An invaluable form that tracks the contract's money, time and Change Orders. Filled out and mailed to GC's home on Monday, includes recent draws.

If I don't use the Contract Tracking I lose focus. I imagine the GC also does. I hand him a copy on Friday and go over it with him.

C) **CONTRACTOR NEGOTIATIONS AND DECISIONS:** On all decisions on money, including Change Orders, I do not agree on a price, time extensions or anything substantial, when I am with the contractor. I discuss and write down everything. I make decisions away from the contractor's influence, pressure or salesmanship. I can be and have been sold. Sometimes, if time is important, I will call him within an hour with a price or "last offer". Other times I wait days. I don't want to regret a quick decision. I have a process and I follow it. So should you.

D) **PRICE LIST OF WHAT I PAY:** Part of my Specification of Material and Methods is an ever-growing price list on what I pay contractors, electricians, plumbers, HVAC and roofers for doing a task. Examples for a plumber: replace a hot water tank, replace a shower diverter, replace a kitchen faucet and trap. Examples for a roofer: install vinyl siding per square, install shingles per square, put on a 16'x50 flat roof with a silvercoat, take out and put in a window and cap the outside etc. It's immensely helpful as I use the list as my "This is the price I pay. Period." Of course the price must be wholesale, good for you and good enough for the contractor to make money.

E) **INSPECT THE WORK BEFORE PAYING**: When I don't inspect Maintenance Request work before I pay, sometimes I regret it. Inspect with punch list in hand, actually two punch lists with carbon paper between. Expect to find things that need correcting. Point them out and write them down. Avoid arguments. Write them down in detail as to their location (2nd floor master bedroom) and specifically what needs to be done. Then hand it to the contractor and go over it in detail. If he says it's "not part of the contract" disagree and continue. Punch lists backed by money wins.

Example: We had a substantial roof leak which caused a bedroom ceiling to come down and the rug was ruined. Six months earlier, I paid for a new flat roof and silvercoat but I was too busy to inspect. No new roof was put on. Only the silvercoat.

I know it may be inconvenient, a hassle, you don't have time, you are not knowledgeable. Doesn't matter. Do it. Inspect all jobs before paying. And only pay when it's 100% done. Not 98% - 100%.

F) HOW TO FIND AND SCREEN POTENTIAL HANDYMEN: Essentially Craigslist, using the same process as the GC Day. Very specific ad. Includes criteria: Live within 10 miles of my home/office or in the area of our houses, minimum 10 years experience, car/truck/van with current driver's license, $12-15 per hour but many times we work by job, minimum of three references. Ask that they reply by email with their phone number and town where they live. Put in your email address. Most don't have resumes. That's okay because with the emailed replies you get a feel for them. Call those that fit your criteria and invite them to your Handyman's Day.

Hold the Handyman's Day at your home/office, or a small Tenant Turnover Rehab, appointments every 30 minutes. They show, hand them the Contractor Application. When they fill it out, go over it with them. If possible photocopy their current driver's license. Are their references friends? Relatives? Or actual customers? How long ago? What was the job? How much? Call references. Visit one job. Own a truck/car/van/minivan? Married? How long? Own or rent a house? Watch yourself. Spend time up front so you don't waste it later. Make haste, slowly. If you find a good one, treat him well but be careful. If the door is open they will walk through it. Try a new one out on a job, if he screws up the first one, he'll screw up the second.

FLASHBACKS OF CONTRACTOR CATASTROPHES.

(Property # refer to those in Chapter Twenty)

Property #1 Hired low bid GC, worked 2-3 days, got paid, no show 2-3 days, great soap opera stories with Runyonesque characters, referrals were buddies from drug rehab, inspector laughed, he's a drug addict, fired him, rehab cost 2 ½ times budget.

Property #2 Hired talkative GC, little progress, went to property unannounced, found GC drunk and asleep on kitchen floor, fired him but he somehow convinced me to pay him for that day.

Property #5 Hired low bid GC, angry when I paid him bid price, entered house at night smashed 2nd floor toilet, it overflowed for 24 hours, 2 a.m. phone call, ceiling on 1st floor down, three feet of water in the basement. $6,000.

Property #12 Personable Irish guy and brother quoted rehab at $9 hour, progressed slow, had family troubles. I pick up newspaper, Mr. Personable was on the front page, killed divorcing wife with knife, pleaded guilty, in jail for life.

Property #16 GC did rehab, pleaded me to rent the rehab to him, wife, three kids, did credit, criminal and eviction check: he had three evictions, wife four. They kept putting off the Home Visit, she was blonde, cute, and so nice. I demanded 1st month rent and two months security deposit. Six months later, three months behind, I evict, fill up a 40 yard dumpster with their trash, house needed an extensive Tenant Turnover Rehab, 3 months to re-rent. $10,000.

Property #24 Joe Cheapskate (me) manages crew, foreman Robert, trust him with a Home Depot credit card, monthly statement comes, see copper charges daily and increasing, confront him, says he's on crack cocaine, I "911", he runs. $8,700 Home Depot copper bill, luckily Home Depot fraud insurance covered it.

Property #26 Hired GC, one price covered labor and materials, excuses, personal tragedies, pleads $8,000 for material to finish, give check, gone forever with my tools.

Property #30 Hired GC who owned /managed rental houses, checked his references, behind on work, no pay, he screams over the phone, came to my house, argued, left, stole tools and jack hammer ($800), two months delay. $4,000

Property Sold/Flipped Second and last contract for labor and materials, (got screwed on both) intelligent and persuasive General Contractor, rehab starts, GC falls/dislocates shoulder, work behind but I make several draw payments, GC needs $7,500, I pay but he doesn't buy material, little progress, asks for another $7,500, I bring wife, good at arguing, shouting match, we leave, that night he steals my building material, toilets, vanities, mirrors, light fixtures and hardwood flooring, I sue, he hires a lawyer, I don't (mistake), he wins, delays 2 months to finish, the full catastrophe costs $20,000. I sell it later and I am able to break even.

Chapter Fifteen

Tenant Choice and Management

Friendly but FIRM

Niche rentals are the foundation for good tenant choice. We offer houses in short supply with strong tenant demand. We let the supply and demand imbalance work for us, not against us. Would you rather attempt to rent a 3 bedroom house in a poor school district (war zone), and have 25 similar houses on Craigslist and in the paper? If you are on the wrong end of the Supply/Demand fulcrum the road is a steep, crater filled, army obstacle course. Phone doesn't ring, open houses sparsely attended, quality of prospective tenants poor as you continue to pay PITI, electric, water, heat, advertise, your time. Frustration sets in. "To hell with it!" You lease to a tenant you shouldn't because you have 1 application, not 6 as we do. You aren't able to follow the guidelines for good Tenant Choice, try as you might, because tenants don't want your house. The newsletters, books and courses on renting techniques, marketing tricks and free months "giveaways" don't help if you are swimming against high supply and low demand. Lower your rental price, give 1st month free, accept half a month's security deposit. All downhill. All based on Supply and Demand.

I go through a careful and patient tenant choice because I have 6 applications. Tenants want what I have. There is limited supply. I choose the tenant that qualifies according to my criteria. Six applications is my trump card.

Within a strong niche, I find that successful tenant management is not difficult. Days go by and I don't receive a call from my tenants. And I don't call them chasing rent. Here's how:

- Careful and patient Tenant Choice.
- Strong Landlord Lease covering everything imaginable (seven parts, 29 pages!)
- Understand, follow, and enforce the lease. (Nice guys finish last!)[*]

---

[*] Leo Durocher, Manager NY Giants and Brooklyn Dodgers

CAREFUL AND PATIENT TENANT CHOICE

Many intelligent investors buy houses well, rehab competently, deal with contractors, have good financing but are horrible, really a zero, at Tenant Choice and Management. Let's go through the system of Tenant Choice.

A house is vacant, Tenant Turnover Rehab is complete. The refinished hardwood floors gleam, white semi-gloss paint everywhere, kitchen and bathroom are spotless, everything clean, clean, clean.

Run below ad in local paper, a more wordy ad on Craigslist (ads/words are free on Craigslist). Craigslist ads are current only one day - therefore we run them 3 x week, generally from different email addresses because Craigslist doesn't like repeat ads.

Town, 4Bd, 2 BA, Beautiful, Gas, Hd FL, FIN BS,

Open House 9/17, 9/29, 10/1 at 6 PM sharp, 427 Stouffer Road

$1275 mo, Section 8 OK, your first name, cell phone #

Meaningful amenities such as a large fenced back yard (FN BK YD), and back deck (BK DK), I abbreviate. I do not waste my time with individual appointments who may or may not show up. Plus competition from other tenants is good for the prospective tenants motivation. No one likes to lose. Notice the Open House has three dates all at 6 p.m. sharp, not 6-8. If no one is there by 6:30, I leave.

THE PHONE CALL

All the information necessary to attend the Open House is in the ad but they still call. I am friendly, upbeat; ask questions to discover if they are the one I'm looking for.

1. "Do you pay regular or have a voucher"? I'm asking if they are Section 8.
   If they have a voucher: "How many bedrooms on the voucher"? Need a four or five corresponding to the property.

2. "Do you have a Landlord Lease Packet"? With it, they have been approved by Section 8 to move.

3. "Have you mailed your 60 day notice?" If they don't have a Landlord Lease Packet and haven't sent their landlord the 60 day notice they're not moving for 70-90 days.

4. If they ask directions, I ask them "Do you have a car?" "Have a GPS?" "Do you have access to MapQuest?" I try to put directions on them. If not, I answer best I can.

All callers are invited to the Open House. All, regardless.

I am looking for a four-bedroom voucher with a Landlord Lease Packet in hand. Perhaps only one out of ten or fifteen phone prospects meets this criteria. If a good prospect calls, I write a 1 next to their name, phone number, and identifying information. I sell the house, i.e. beautiful, two bathrooms, hardwood floors, good school district, near public transportation.

With a few prospects we "connect." They are intelligent, excited. "Call me Joe," I say to make the process personal. I may call a very good prospect the day of the Open House to confirm. If they don't show, I call and find out why.

TEACHING POINT: My cell phone is DHR's business phone. All calls come to me. Bad? No, good. We train, and our lease mandates, that our tenants DO NOT call except in emergencies which are defined in the lease. We communicate in writing, through the mail. I answer my phone selectively and call back selectively. I am in control. On vacation I hand the phone to an associate. What could be simpler?

THE OPEN HOUSE

I arrive 15 minutes early. Put For Rent sign on the front lawn--4 bedrooms, $1,275 mo, in black magic marker. Our made-to-last signs, real steel legs, already have FOR RENT and my cell phone number.

I walk through the house, open doors and windows for fresh air, put on lights. Set up a fold-up table with 4 steel chairs, applications, pens and sign-in book.

As they enter I stand, greet them, get their name, ask them to sign in. "Look around. Feel free. Basement is finished, a bedroom, den and bathroom." I point to the basement door.

If I really like them and I'm not busy, I may tag along pointing out this and that, asking questions, getting to know them, low key.

After they have looked through I ask EVERYONE, "Would you like to fill out an application?"

Why do I invite EVERYONE to attend the Open House and fill out an application? A cautionary step to ensure that no government spy would accuse me of prejudice against a protected class. You never know - so I ask EVERYONE.

APPLICATION

"Is there an application fee?"

"Yes, a million dollars," I answer. Laughter. "No application fee," I tell them.

Why? My prospective tenants don't have a lot of cash. I don't run credit/eviction/criminal checks ($25 cost) until they pass the Home Visit, so why have obstacles? I want applications. A full four pages takes them 20 to 30 minutes to fill out. Great starting point.

"Can I take it with me?"

"No. We have to witness the signature." Nineteen out of twenty applications given out you will never see again. If they are excited and motivated they will stay and fill out the application. If they are not, they will not rent from you.

"My credit isn't good."

"We understand spotty credit. Any evictions? If not, you are fine." With Section 8 poor credit isn't a major factor. Section 8 pays the major portion and we have found that Section 8 tenants will pay their share.

Some struggle with the application, some dash through, some ask questions. If they start, they generally finish.

When they finish I say, "Let me go over this with you." I go over the entire application line by line. I tell them to call me with a landlord's phone number or other missing information. The application is very thorough. I ask questions, make notes and write the information needed right on the application (some experts advise against, phooey!) and try to understand their situation. I know a good deal about the prospect when I finish. I write a "general impression" number from 1 to 5 on the top of the application. 1 is excellent, 5 is run-for-the-hills bad.

HOW TO ASSESS A SECTION 8 PROSPECT AT THE OPEN HOUSE

1. Number of bedrooms on voucher? Do they have or when will they receive a Landlord Lease Packet? Sent their mandatory 60 day certified letter to their current Landlord? Or are they waiting "till I get a house?" When can they move?

2. How long with Section 8? How many times have they moved? How long do they want to rent for? On our application they choose 12–24–36–48 mos. I want those that circle 48 months or write longer! Tenant Turnover is the number one expense!

3. Kids. Open and friendly or sullen and withdrawn? Ages of kids. Young is good. Teenage not so. Angry teenage males blah.

4. Cooperative or belligerent? Neat or sloppy? Intelligent or slow? A mover or a stayer?

5. Does the prospect want the house? Some salivate. It's their dream home. Are they anxious about losing it?

    "When will I hear if I have the house?" or "How long does the application process take?"

    "We process applications in 3 days. The investors then make the decision."

If the prospect qualifies I set up a Home Visit at that time, or at the latest the next day. I focus on the qualified prospect which is Section 8, four bedroom voucher, Landlord Lease packet in hand. I want that prospect processed within three days. The Home Visit is the key.

TEACHING POINT: **THE INVESTORS** are the behind-the-scene power. Blame them for everything. They decide everything. The investors this, the investors that.

"Why was my application turned down?" "The investors didn't say why."

"Can you delete these late charges?" "The investors won't let us do that."

"Why can't I have a small dog?" "The investors don't want pets."

"Why did you file for eviction in District Court?" "The investors decided that."

Takes you off the point. My card says Manager. I refer to myself as Manager. Easier for me to deliver bad news without beating around the bush. I don't care if they know I'm the Owner/Landlord. No one has ever confronted me. Having investors to blame makes my job easier.

THE HOME VISIT

With Section 8 tenants having the Fed paying most of the rent, this eliminates the need for good credit, the major criteria for cash tenants. The Home Visit becomes the major event in the application process (I don't do home visits with students). What you see and smell at a home visit is what your house will be like after 30 days. It's that simple. Never pass over the Home Visit. I know it's inconvenient, time consuming and possibly intrusive on you and the prospective tenant. Having done home visits for years, **I WOULD NEVER, EVER LET A TENANT IN WITHOUT ONE.** I am astounded why all landlords don't make home visits mandatory.

Expect 33% of prospective tenants will not make an appointment, cancel, not answer the phone on your confirmation call one hour before the visit or not answer the door. They know what their house is like. They are avoiding the expected rejection. So be it.

HOW TO CONDUCT A HOME VISIT

1) MAKE AN APPOINTMENT immediately or at a maximum within 2 days of the application. Why? Gives them less time to clean and throw out junk. Confirm by phone one hour before. You don't want to waste your time. If they put you off they are generally cleaning or are embarrassed by what you will find.

2) ARRIVE ON TIME: How is the block? Junk in front yard? Grass cut? Front door damaged? Sheets hanging in windows? Piles of garbage bags on curb? Guess where that came from? Look down driveway, side yard for junk, furniture, pets.

3) SMILE AND BE FRIENDLY: Door opens, how's the smell? Put them at ease. Walk in. Are the kids open? Smile? Sullen? I ask their names, engage them "Do you play sports?" Windows sheets/blankets? Rug dirty? "Do you have a vacuum?" (some don't, it's broken, etc.) Neat? Orderly? Holes in walls, ceiling? Kitchen clean? Stove? Open the oven. Floor? Cockroaches?

4) UPSTAIRS: Rugs on stairs? Bathroom a mess? Tub? Open the door of each bedroom, if one is locked ask them to get the key. If they can't find/doesn't have key, something is behind that door they don't want you to see. I don't expect kids' rooms to be neat but not a catastrophe, master bedroom, this is their space.

5) BASEMENT: Yes go down, regardless of all, no lights? I carry a flashlight. Washer and dryer hookup? Storage? Total disaster? Do you want your basement to look like this?

6) BACKYARD: If you can see from the kitchen fine, if not, go around house, sometimes it's a mess, junk everywhere. Once I found a dog tied up with bruise marks.

7) LANDLORD REPAIRS: If the house needs a rehab, walls brown, rugs a mess, holes in walls, doors hanging on one hinge; the tenant may blame the slumlord, who is horrible and does absolutely nothing! I have found that good tenants have good landlords and good houses. Junky tenants have junky landlords and junky houses. No.

8) SLAM DUNK: You walk in, neat as a pin, room after room, everything perfect, nicer/neater than your house! Quick do a credit, eviction and criminal check. Call them back within an hour, "You have the house. I'd like to come over and pick up the security deposit." Money talks loudly as to their commitment.

9) GIVE A NUMBER: Each Home Visit gets a number (1 - excellent, 2 - good, 3 - fair, 4 - poor, 5 - run for the hills bad) written on their Home Visit Checklist. You now have 2 numbers, one from the Open House and Application, the second from the Home Visit. Both the same? We don't rent to those below 2.

10) THE CLOSE: We held the Open Houses, have 6 applications but like one a lot. One or two days later, the Home Visit, if they pass we run the credit, eviction (we don't want tenants with eviction filings) and criminal check. Call the current and past landlords. We let the facts make our decision. Don't worry or get anxious. Follow the system. Nine out of 10 times the facts will make the decision for you. Let's say you have 5 other good applications in process. Do you wait for the 5 others to be completed and choose the best one, or do you pull the trigger on the 1st one that completes your process and qualifies. Immediately pull the trigger on the 1st one as long as they score a 1 on both. If they are a 2, is there a 1 in your prospect mix? The Home Visit number is much more important than the Application number. We want a number 1. Will settle for a number 2. We don't rent to a 3.

I call, congratulate the tenant for being approved, go over the move-in date, make the appointment to quickly pick up the Landlord Lease Packet. I also ask for the required rental deposit (turns into the security deposit after tenant moves in) of $1275. Ah ha! Money! Says they don't have $1275 but would $700 down with the rest paid off monthly be OK. I accept (we don't take less than $500 down) and make an appointment for tomorrow at 7 pm at their current home at which time:

1. I pick up the Landlord Lease Packet.

2. Fill out Required Rental Deposit (Part 6 of Lease) for the $700 and fill in the dates they commit to mail (postmark date is the date of payment) the remainder of the rental deposit at $100 or more per month.

3. Return to office, fill out Landlord Lease Packet and return it to tenant. I monitor their appointment with the caseworker assigned to handle all DHR tenants. We are big enough to have one case manager handle all our properties. Very helpful.

4. Tenant makes appointment with caseworker who approves the lease, the packet enclosures and rental amount. Tenant signs our lease. Tenant leaves and calls me with the good news.

If prospect does not give me the required rental deposit or procrastinates for any reason, I move to another prospect. First come, first served. Other qualified and approved prospects not getting the house will be routed to other houses we may have, or be put on hold. It is not unusual for us to move a prospect to another house. Sometimes we even rent houses sight unseen, as when a house is under rehab. "All our houses are rehabbed the same way, all are beautiful!", we tell the prospect. We have a book with very powerful and effective before and after pictures of rehabs. They may have seen one, liked it a lot and lost it. They don't want to lose another.

MORE DOS AND DON'TS

1) DON'T ALLOW SLOBS: THINK HOME VISIT!

A) They destroy your house. When they leave, (evicted or voluntarily) the Tenant Turnover Rehab is extensive. Lots of money. Lots of time.

B) They have relatives, boyfriends, etc. living there.

C) Don't like living in their own filth and move.

D) Family fights, police incident reports, fights with neighbors, relatives.

E) They fight the eviction and prolong the process because other landlords are too intelligent to take them in. They have nowhere to go.

2) DON'T HOTELS/MOTELS/HOMELESS/MOTHER/SISTER'S/HOUSES/ SAINTLY STATE SOCIAL AGENCIES/PLEASE/PLEASE LET ME IN!

All prospective tenants who live in the above have valid reasons, and absolutely none are their fault. All their reasons, stories and dramas end badly. For you. Because they don't pay. DON'T PAY. PROBLEMS. SLOBS. Remember, you're a landlord not a social worker.

3) DON'T ALLOW EVICTIONS OR EVICTION FILINGS ON REPORT: ONE IS TOO MANY!

A) Tenant has 2 evictions on report, but wonderful stories exonerating her, actually making her the heroine. I let her in, she falls asleep, stove fire, $40,000 in damages.

B) Personable husband (3 eviction filings), vivacious wife (4 eviction filings), they put off, put off, I never did the home visit. I was impatient and stupid, they gave me 2 months security deposit. Six months later I evicted them, house full junk/garbage, filled a 40 yard, 8' high dumpster, major rehab followed.

C) If they have one eviction, it's one too many. They now know the rules, work the system, show up in court, prolong, maybe get a Legal Aide free lawyer. DON'T.

4) DON'T ALLOW DRUGS, ALCOHOL, PAROLE

A mere hint of drugs is too much. Part of my Rental Application is the question "Will you and your household submit now or during the lease, to a drug test?" They all answer YES. Good. If you have an indication of any kind that there are drugs involved have them submit to a "hair" drug test - it's the Gold Standard- costs $75. I use it. You are not AA.

Tenants on parole? Wonderful, dress up as a warden for your lease signing. No.

5) DO THE 7-PART LEASE AND MOVE IN

The Landlord Lease Packet comprises Part 1 of our lease which I and the prospect sign and initial. Back at the office I photocopy it twice for a total of 3 copies, one for Section 8, one for tenant, one for DHR. I add a Certificate of Occupancy from the municipality, and a property settlement sheet proving I own the property. Get the packet back to the tenant ASAP.

The 7-Part Lease comprises the foundation of the landlord/tenant relationship. Contains all the rules, obligations and penalties. Tenant management can be defined as enforcing what the lease says which the tenant has agreed to. This is what I try to do. I have slowly expanded the lease to the current 25 pages so it covers every conceivable possibility. These are the rules I enforce.

Part I – "Lease Terms", 13 pages. Tenant initials each page and signs last page. If I hadn't done so at the first signing because of time constraints, I read each paragraph and ask for questions. The paragraphs are numbered 1-58 and cover 99% of what might happen during the lease. From the time when a payment is late, date when Pay or Move form is sent, to the allowable length of the grass (5") it's all there. Very inclusive.

Part II – "Lead Paint", 1 page. Tenant signs bottom of Disclosure of Information on Lead-Based Paint Hazards.

Part III – "Utility Turn On", 2 pages. Tenant initials throughout and signs bottom of second page. We circle the utilities that service the house. Contains utilities requirements and their phone numbers, move in date from which tenant is responsible.

Following utilities are placed in tenant's name:

1) Electric

2) Gas turn on. If natural gas is not available we use propane.

3) Water turn on.

4) Sewer, we pay. Some municipalities have sewer as a flat fee, some have the sewer based on water usage.

Part IV – "Tenant Move In/Landlord Move Out Inventory Check List".

Section A: 4 pages. Tenant signs last page. Tenant walks through house, notes problems on sheet, very inclusive. Same form is used by landlord when tenant moves.

Section B: 1 page, Price List of house items. Tenant signs bottom.

Comprehensive list of prices if, upon tenant moving out, or before, house has items or materials that are broken, missing, misused or must be replaced, above normal wear and tear.

Part V – "Maintenance Request", 3 pages, 1st page an explanation of DHRs Maintenance Request Policy. Tenant initials each paragraph and signs bottom.

2nd and 3rd pages are 2 copies of DHR's Maintenance Request which is, for Tenant's convenience, also mailed to Tenant with each monthly statement.

Part VI – "Required Rental Deposit", 1 page. Tenant signs on bottom.

Acknowledgement that tenant has given a rental deposit, which will be credited to security deposit, upon tenant possession. Gives a dated payment schedule if one is needed to complete the balance. Last paragraph "How to Get Full Return of the Security Deposit" which mirrors the language in the lease and the letter we send to tenant when we are notified tenant is moving out.

Part VII – "Highlights of Lease", 2 pages. I read aloud and explain each paragraph, then ask for questions. If none, the tenant initials that paragraph. I then move on to the next. These 30 paragraphs are the most common areas of lease violations. When a lease is violated I mail the form Notice of Lease Violation on which the violation is written in detail, time frame to correct, if not corrected the premises must be vacated by_____. Also included is a photocopy of the appropriate page of Highlights of Lease, with that paragraph and tenants initials highlighted in orange. The tenant has no place to go.

After the entire teaching and signing session, the tenant walks through the house and fills out Part IV Tenant Move In Inventory. I then give the tenant the key, along with flowers or another house warming gift and congratulate the new tenant. Their dream house is theirs. (Delco Home Rentals' motto is "Dream Houses for Rent".)

TEACHING POINT – Time of year families/students move? Short answer – summer. Families move to register their kids in the new school district. Students move to get situated for class and activities such as sports. July and August are the most active. Bookends are June and September. Aim your purchases, rehabs, voluntary move outs and evictions to correspond to the demand in the summer months. Summer is a hustle depending on how many new houses and tenant turnovers you have.

Chapter Sixteen

Smart Rental Rehabs

Introducing the Eliminators!

If you are a mechanical klutz, still trying to figure out which way the screw turns, don't like to get your hands dirty and have never owned a battery powered tool, I have good news. It's okay. You're like me. You can hire folks to do those things, who actually LIKE to do those things and who LOVE their tools like you love your pet. Glad you're over that hump?

Specification of Material and Methods is Exhibit B of my 7-part Independent Contractors Services Agreement which includes all information you need to manage the following:

1. Rehab a property.

2. Tenant turnover rehab.

3. Maintenance requests.

I must admit I am proud of this very comprehensive Specification of Material and Methods. I believe a novice investor can, with the Specification in hand, do rehabs and maintenance requests well and inexpensively.

The Specification lists all items (light fixtures, stove, mini blinds, etc) and material (paint, drywall) to be used including the SKU#s from Home Depot. Explains what items go where, sometimes a 1st and 2nd choice if Home Depot is out of choice 1. Includes prices you should pay plumbers, electricians, hardwood refinishers, ceramic tile mechanics, HVAC technicians, roofers and handymen. It's a mini how-to book.

The 7-part Independent Contractor Services Agreement is (including the Specification) 39 pages; Residential Lease, 7 part, 25 pages; Tenant Application, 4 pages; and approximately 100 other real estate forms I use cannot fit in this book. They are covered in detail in Chapter 21.

The **ELIMINATORS!** is my favorite chapter in the Specification. It lists items that SHOULD NOT be included in your rental house. It will save you thousands of dollars. If I had the 7-part Independent Contractor Services Agreement, including the Specification of Material and Methods, when I started, along with Chapter 14, Contractors from Hell! I would have saved an enormous amount of time, pain and thousands and thousands of dollars.

Our motto is "Dream Homes for Rent" and as our pictures illustrate, we deliver on that promise. But we also have to make money. So we ELIMINATE those items that are commonly mistreated, broken, wear out, disappear, then are repaired or replaced by us. When you rehab, you don't install the ELIMINATORS! If it's already there, you ELIMINATE it. If it's there at a Tenant Turnover Rehab, ELIMINATE it. If you get a maintenance request (MR) or if it's broken during an inspection, don't fix, ELIMINATE! If the ELIMINATORS! aren't there, there will not be maintenance requests to repair them. Make it simple. ELIMINATE the maintenance request before it occurs! Save money, save time and stay sane!

ELIMINATORS!

Things We Do <u>NOT</u> Have In Our Rental Houses

1.) Carpet - no carpet at all – zero - refinish the hardwood, ceramic the rest.

2.) Regular battery operated smoke detectors. Gone. Home Depot sells a Lithium battery smoke detector guaranteed to last 10 years. Buy it.

3.) Ceiling fans

4.) Dishwashers. Don't fix, throw out. Put in a kitchen cabinet.

5.) Central air - $3000 to replace? No. Tenants use window air conditioner units.

6.) Trees, bushes, shrubs. Take them out. Tenants don't take care of them.

7.) Doorbells.

8.) Screen door or storm door. Don't fix, throw out.

9.) Closet doors. broken, bi folds? Replace with nothing.

10.) Fluorescent lights in basement. Don't fix, eliminate! Use flush mounted HD lights.

11.) Toilet paper holders, towel racks.

12.) Torn screens – Fix with kit, or in a pinch use $4 accordion screens

13.) Radiator covers. Not necessary according to code.

14.) Windows:

> a. Code mandates one window per room, eliminate all but one window on porches and basements; all gone in sheds, garages.

b. In rehab, eliminate old windows with new well made vinyl double hung. Old windows don't lock, stay up or pass inspection.

15.) Hose bibs (faucets) on outside walls of house.

16.) Five gallon flush toilet. Replace with 1.6 Kohler Wellworth.

17.) Basement - Eliminate all wires, nails, shelves, appliances, trash, boards, old oil tanks, Bilco doors, everything.

18.) Awnings.

19.) Built-in microwaves.

20.) Roof antennas.

21.) Wooden decks. If on 1st floor, can replace with a cement patio.

22.) Fences: Vinyl picket fence with missing pickets, kids pull them off, or old wooden picket fence needs maintenance, best fence is no fence. Need a fence? Cyclone, lasts a generation.

23.) Oil Furnaces. Replace with natural gas or propane, Gas has no MR's.

24.) Shower glass doors. They come off the runners and they leak. Use a rod and a full curtain with liner. If necessary, put a shag rug to soak up water.

25.) Replace 2-handle faucets, standardize on 1 lever Moen cartridge faucet from plumbing supply (higher quality, slightly higher price) not Home Depot.

26.) Garbage disposals.

27.) Refrigerator, washer and dryer. Tenant brings and maintains their own appliances (except stove.) But include if you rent to students.

28.) Broken concrete that is not needed, take up, seed grass or stone.

29.) Garage walk-in door/windows. Have one roll-up garage door, no windows.

30.) Six panel door, if tenant breaks a few 6-panel doors, replace door with solid wood door. 6-panel doors, however are our specification standard.

31.) Drop ceilings.

32.) Paneling - Take out or paint white, drywall over bad walls, ceilings.

33.) Land line telephone wires are out. Leave in cable or dish if working.

34.) Wall paper, best to take it off. If layered install 3/8 drywall over it.

35.) Exposed outside wood: Cap aluminum. Once and Done. All of it.

36.) Cabinet knobs.

37.) Dimmer switches.

38.) Kitchen sink sprayer, buy one hole sink at plumbers supply, not Home Depot.

39.) Shutters.

40.) Slag (pebbles) flat roof, hot (kettle) roof. Instead use torch down rubber flat roof.

41.) Fuses/old small electric panel, replace 30 slot Siemens, Home Depot.

42.) Basement commercial tile, take up, paint cement floor gray.

The Eliminators! = No Maintenance Requests or phone calls. Quiet. Silent Night 24/7. Almost Holy.

FORMULA FOR REHABS

During a rehab I attempt to solve all future maintenance requests for the next twenty years and finance the costs in the permanent financing mortgage- currently amortized over 20 years. Realistically, I know I will have maintenance requests, but I attempt to shut out the majority of them during the rehab.

1. Have a plan for 4TH or 5TH bedroom.
2. Demo it, eliminate the ELIMINATORS!
3. Lawn, cut bushes, trees.
4. Plumbing- replace faucets with Moen single lever cartridge. Replace corroded pipes with PVC or Pex.
5. Basement water- possible French drain or sump pumps.
6. Electrical- 30 slot Siemens panel from Home Depot- replace all knob and tube wiring. 2 outlets per room, by code, all work by code and inspected.
7. Windows- if they are old wooden windows, replace with double hung vinyl windows.
8. Kitchen – Paint or refinish, or replace cabinets.
9. Replace light fixtures (flush mounted, $10 at Home Depot) as needed.
10. Spackle and caulk are your friends.
11. Paint it all with MAB semi-gloss, extra white.
12. Flooring- Refinish hardwood, ceramic floors in kitchen, bath and every other place that is not hardwood.
13. Smoke detectors with a 10 year warranty, Mini blinds on all windows.

14. Silvercoat (elastomer) flat roof.

15. Heat- if oil, replace with gas.

16. Washer and dryer outlets- install with dryer outlet to outside.

17. Clean, clean, clean after the hardwood is refinished.

HOW REHABS PAY ME $2+ FOR EVERY $1 SPENT

My rehabs don't cost me money, they make me money. For every $1 spent on a rehab I create $2+ in Forced Appreciation. Here is how it works.

For this example: Appraisal: $100,000;   Purchase Price: $40,000;

Settlement costs: $5,000; Rehab Costs: $25,000

1. FIRST FIND OUT HOW MUCH MORE THE APPRAISAL IS THAN WHAT YOU SPENT

Appraisal After Rehab
−(Puchased Price and Settlement Costs)
= Forced Appreciation or Increased Value

$100,000
−($40,000 *and* $5,000)
= $55,000

---

2. THEN FIND OUT THE RATIO OF WHAT YOU SPENT TO THE INCREASE IN VALUE

$Rehab\ Costs\sqrt{Forced\ Appreciation}$
= Ratio of Forced Appreciation to Each Dollar Spent

$\$25,000\sqrt{\$55,000}$ = **$2.20**

Get it? For every dollar you spent on rehab, you increased the value of the rehabbed home by $2.20. You more than doubled your money! Plus a rehabbed property is easier to rent and has fewer maintenance requests!

On the Pre-Offer Property Worksheet there is an easy, follow-the-dots formula for estimating Forced Appreciation. Our *standard* is $2 and our *goal* is $3 in Forced Appreciation. I then attempt to add the rehab cost into my long-term financing. If you finance 100% of the rehab cost you have created the Forced Appreciation from your brain/sweat equity.

FORCED APPRECIATION EXAMPLES FROM CHAPTER TWENTY

Example A: #32 in Chapter Twenty:

After Rehab Appraisal		$135,000
Minus Sale Price	-	$ 64,000
Minus Settlement Costs	-	$ 5,300
Forced Appreciation		$ 65,700
Divided by Rehab Cost		$ 27,000 = $2.43 dollars for every dollar spent

Example B: #44 in Chapter Twenty:

After Rehab Appraisal		$120,000
Minus Sale Price	-	$ 40,000
Minus Settlement Costs	-	$ 3,581
Forced Appreciation		$ 76,419
Divided by Rehab Costs		$ 36,500 = $2.09 dollars for every dollar spent

Example C: #48 in Chapter Twenty

After Rehab Appraisal		$125,000
Minus Sale Price	-	$ 35,000
Minus Settlement Costs	-	$ 5,000
Forced Appreciation		$ 85,000
Divided by Rehab Costs		$ 35,000 = $2.42 dollars for every dollar spent

CAN'T STOP, HERE'S MORE FORCED APPRECIATION!

During a rehab in which you take a 3 bedroom, 1 bath house and finish the basement with a 4th bedroom, powder room and a den, upgrade from oil to gas heat, replace the electrical panel and wiring, refinish the hardwood and install ceramic in the kitchen, bathroom and any room without hardwood, you have radically changed the value of that house in several ways.

1) An investor will pay more for the house because, instead of renting a three bedroom for $1050, the four bedroom is renting for $1,300, which increases the Net by 166%! What is that worth to an investor buyer?

2) A future primary home buyer will pay more for the 40% increase in the basement living space and the powder room.

3) Let's take one of my very recent purchases - a 3 bedroom, 1 bath with a large (12x24) single garage in a good school district. We transform it into a 5 bedroom, 1.5 bath ($1400 month rent) and garage with electric ($200 month rent) for a total of $1600. If you sold the property to an investor, he would be collecting $1600 instead of $1050 for a three bedroom and that extra $550 goes straight to the bottom line. Has to be worth an additional $30,000 to the sale price.

The thing I love about real estate is there are so many creative and fun ways to make money!

Before and After Rehab

Before and After Rehab

Chapter Seventeen

Leverage And The Push Up Bra

How To Make A Little Look Like A Lot

"Tom, fantastic ocean view. It's like having your own private beach." I sat comfy warm looking through sliding glass at a beautifully desolate ocean in winter.

"Off season is best. No crowds."

"Later we'll walk the beach?"

"Sure, the wife and kids love it. Have to button up. Wind goes right through you."

"Tom, not to be nosy but how do you afford this?" He was a sales guy, wife stayed home with three young kids, figured he didn't earn over $60,000.

Tom laughed. "I couldn't even afford to rent the damn thing during the summer. I get $6,000 a week during July and August, less in June and September and some holidays."

"But how did you buy it?

"Bank financed 80% LTV over 30 years at 5.5%. The seller was absolutely desperate to get out. . . so we offered and she agreed to take back a sweet 2nd mortgage to replace the 20% down payment, no interest for 6 months then interest only for 5 yrs at, get this, 4%."

"So how much did you have to bring to settlement?"

"Nothing. Settled May 31st. Got all the summer deposits. Walked out of settlement with $6,500."

"That's amazing! But what happens after 5 years?"

"Sell it. I can't afford to live in it. Or rent it." Tom laughed, shrugged his shoulders. "It's crazy."

The Deal		Funny Money Financing	Total Financed	Monthly Payments
Purchase Price	1,000,000	1st Mtg 80% LTV 30 yrs 5.5%	800,000	4,800 mo
Settlement Costs	30,000	2nd Mtg 20% LTV 4% 5yr balloon	200,000	660 mo
		Summer Rental Deposits	36,500	Total 5,460 mo
Total Cost	1,030,000	Total Received	1,036,500	Rent 5,200 mo Avg
		Minus Total Cost	-1,030,000	-260 mo Loss
		Into Tom's Pocket	+ 6,500	

UNDERSTANDING "FUNNY MONEY"

Everyone thinks they understand money. It's the stuff we earn then buy things with. True but what is it?

Money is a recent invention. During 99% of Homosapiens' stay on earth, money, in any form, did not exist. We were hunters and gatherers and negotiated and traded goods and services in our tribe/group. Sam, a hunter, killed a deer, brought it to Walter the first butcher, who cut it up and kept 10% for his services. The trade opportunities were limited since both parties had to be present and have exactly what the other needed.

Then precious metals (gold, silver) or commonly used goods (tobacco) became an accepted medium of exchange, i.e. money, thus easing trading limitations and increasing its frequency.

Within the last two hundred years, governments intruded into the marketplace with their own FIAT money defined as "state issued legal tender which is neither legally convertible to any other thing, is not fixed in value and has no intrinsic value in terms of any objective standard." The United State's FIAT money is worth whatever the world-wide market thinks it's worth, so the dollar's value goes up and down daily.

For a variety of self-serving reasons, governments gravitated to paper FIAT money. Initially the United States backed its paper currency by the gold standard; that is, every paper dollar had a corresponding amount of gold in "Fort Knox." This barred the Fed from printing money to cover over budget extravagant spending. In 1971 President Nixon moved us off the gold standard which opened the gate for the Fed to print as much as Congress and the President demanded.

Paper money facilitated a dramatic increase in worldwide trading. Governments and businesses then took paper FIAT money ("no intrinsic value") to the next level. Digital. Think about it. Do you pay with cash or a credit card? Do you pay bills "on line"? Are your stocks,

IRA, 401K, mutual funds, ETF's, savings accounts, loans, etc. in paper dollars? No. Digital. The Fed no longer prints. As in Genesis, out of nothing, billions, trillions race light speed to every corner of the World Wide Web. Money is a numerical symbol, with fluctuating worth, and no intrinsic value. Think of it as digital clay in the hands of an artist: you. Call it Funny Money.

The financing of real estate is created with Funny Money. The numbers only obliquely represent real value, like a shadow represents its object. Not the hard-earned green you once spent for food, gas and clothes. Credit cards are Funny Money. Monthly payments are Funny Money. How much is a car? $269 a month. How much is a house? $1200 a month. The deluxe version with a pool? $1,650 a month. Real estate investment financing is a more advanced, you might say a B.S. (Bullshit) in Funny Money. Wall Street has an M.S. (More of Same) and hedge fund managers have a PhD. (Piled High and Deep). Funny Money is an enticing but sometimes dangerous high wire act. Archimedes, centuries ago, said, "Give me a lever long enough, and a fulcrum on which to place it and I shall move the world." Old Archimedes wasn't referring to real estate investment financing, but it's applicable. Financing is your lever to buy, manage and eventually really OWN (or refinance!) the property. Studying, understanding and manipulating Funny Money, you can create financing that gives you what you previously thought impossible. "Creative Financing" says what it means. It's MAGIC! Some things, like David Copperfield, you make disappear. Others you want larger and use funhouse mirrors. The following are the players in the game.

THE BANK

The Bank (bank is generic for mortgage provider) is your must-have slow dance snuggle up partner. She is eternally fickle, depending on your credit score, down payment, ratios, type of property, location, 1040, 1120, cash flow, really everything imaginable. A moving target. Therefore, you must be consistently vigilant of how you look to your provider of real estate newborns. For without financing, ah...where would we be?

Do you need a makeover? Botox, liposuction, exercise, diet, makeup, fine threads, smile pretty, tummy in chest out, toupee, yes to diction lessons! Not quite that kind. But close. You need a financial makeover because a bank loans money only if you prove you don't need it. But hell, they have to lend to someone. That's how they make money! Who better than you and I? Let's see how we can pretty ourselves up with investment financing basics.

INVESTMENT FINANCING BASICS

1. **Monitor, build and protect your credit score**

Go online to AnnualCreditReport.com. You are, by law, allowed one free credit report per year. But you must BUY the Credit Score, which is the number everyone uses to evaluate your credit worthiness.

FIRST STEP, DISPUTE: There are three major credit reporting agencies, TransUnion, Experian and Equifax. Some online sites offer all three reports and I suggest you use them. They will try to sell you a monthly monitoring service for $10-19 a month. The service can be useful as you monitor and build your credit score. I use one. Once you have your three credit reports, there will be a very valuable number on the report to be used as you **DISPUTE** all the negatives online immediately. Don't put it off, **DISPUTE** all negatives on the credit report, immediately, true or not, doesn't matter, you **DISPUTE** them. Disputing online using your credit report number is easy, fast and you get a response quickly. The key is this: Congress passed a law that says when you dispute a negative the company who reported the negative has 30 days to verify the truth of the negative. If from your dispute date they do not respond within 30 days, the credit reporting company **MUST BY LAW DELETE THE NEGATIVE FROM YOUR CREDIT REPORT!** Get it? That's the game. Play it.

Let's say you start with 7 negatives. You dispute all 7. Five report back in 30 days, two don't. You are down to 5. Ninety days later do it again. That's right. Do it again. Then again, etc. If you have paper proof of your claim include that in a mailed dispute but keep a copy. Be a bulldog. Take a bite, hold on, and keep going.

SECOND STEP, PAY ALL YOUR BILLS ON TIME: Pay your credit cards first, hopefully down to zero each month. Credit cards, loans and mortgages all have a grace period. Don't go over that date. Lenders report lateness to the credit bureaus after 30 days.

THIRD STEP, DEBT TO AVAILABLE CREDIT RATIO: An important ratio is your total credit issued versus the credit used. Overall, the lower the ratio the better your score. Staying under 10% owed versus your available credit adds significantly to your score. If your credit cards are maxed out yet you are paying monthly on time, because of the ratio mentioned, your score is lowered.

FOURTH STEP, BUILD CREDIT: Establish higher credit limits on your current credit cards, open other lines of credit, visit and make loans with local banks and credit unions. Build it up slowly. Keep building.

FIFTH STEP, FICO's SCORE SIMULATOR: If you buy your scores on myfico.com they offer a score simulator to play with. You can simulate how your score would react under certain conditions.

If your score needs repair and you aren't organized or disciplined enough to do it, admit it and pay a credit repair company $300/$450 for one year to get it done. It's worth it because you need good credit. It's the ticket to play the game.

Here are two books on the credit game, go on Amazon and price them used.

- From Credit Repair to Credit Millionaire, Donna L. Fox, Esq.
- Credit Scores and Credit Reports, Evan Hendricks.

2. Risk Tolerance

What is your risk tolerance? What is your spouse's risk tolerance? Goes from 0 to 100. Mine's about 95. My spouse's is 10. Sometimes that's a problem. Do you see debt as bad? To be paid off ASAP? Or as a bridge to reach your pot of gold?

I view mortgage debt as a future asset being paid down every month by my wonderful tenants. I see short-term debt (including credit cards) as a temporary bridge to long-term financing. Today's mortgage for investors is generally a 20-year amortization with a 5-year balloon. The 5-year balloon gives the bank an opportunity to reset the rate while charging a fee. If you are current the bank will probably not call the loan. You are a performing asset; they have enough of the other kind.

3. Capital

What capital (cash) do you have to invest? Savings? IRA? 401K? (an IRA and some 401K's may be invested in real estate regardless of what some uninformed people tell you) inheritance, stocks, bonds, mutual funds, ETFs, family members, friends or spouses with cash, rob bank, be a country and print money. Seek and you will find!

4. Lines of Credit

Credit cards? Home equity line of credit (sometimes called a 2nd mortgage) on your current home? Real estate that can be refinanced? Overdraft protection? Autos that are paid for?

A note on credit cards. I have four with a total line of $100,000. Useful. You pay no interest if you pay them off monthly. Good monthly tracking for your expenses. Try low interest cards from local credit unions or USAA if you are ex-military. Go online and troll. Ask for a large credit line if you think you can get it. Starting out? Ask for $5,000. Good credit? $15,000. Excellent credit? $30,000.

Continue to improve your credit score and every six months ask for increases in all your lines of credit. Keep researching and securing lines of credit for future use.

5. Interest Amortization Tables

Buy an interest rate/amortization book or calculator. Use it to calculate your Pre Offer Property Worksheet. I also carry a 3x5 card with the rates and factors. A factor is a number times the principal loaned that gives the monthly payment. I use factors all the time on my Pre Offer Property Worksheet.

Specific Vehicles I have used for Financing

1. Mortgage Broker

A mortgage broker is an independent business person who represents many different banks and mortgage providers. They can pick and choose the right fit for your needs and credit profile. Find an experienced, local, small mortgage broker, with low costs. Ask for and speak with the owner. Make an appointment. Bring all your financial information, i.e., balance sheet (get a blank one online), loans, monthly payments, last two 1040s and W2s, and last three pay stubs. Ask them to pull your credit report/score (brokers can pull your score without the credit bureau knowing) as you sit there. Cut to the chase. Give the owner/agent your Agreement of Sale (AOS) or your plan (buy 3 investment properties in the next 12 months). Brokers don't make money until you settle on a property. They want you to settle!

A good broker has credit software that emulates the FHA's and other lenders' criteria. They input your information, amount of mortgage, and it will reject or accept your pre-application. If rejected they know why and both of you can tweak the obstacles until you are accepted.

Your mortgage broker, especially on an FHA mortgage, is your ticket. Visit and interview at least three. Get referrals from other investors. My broker is very good and inexpensive. If a deal can be done, she can do it. If she can't, she tells me why.

2. Small Commercial Banks

Today this is the best and in some circumstances the only game. On the positive side the bank is local, knows your real estate market, is experienced and comfortable with investor real estate lending. In 2008/09/10 commercial banks are where I have and hopefully will continue to receive financing.

Small commercial banks look more at the property's cash flow than at the owner's credit. If they have to foreclose they want a positive cash flow.

Gaining a referral to the bank from a well thought of investor is best.

3. FHA Home Loan

A) For primary home buyers, 3.5% down, 30 yr amortization, low interest rate. A sweet deal but supposedly only once. If successful try again in 2 years. Best for houses with little or no rehab unless you can buy and rehab with cash, then mortgage with FHA.

B) Get an FHA up front, then after the rehab, pay for an appraisal and apply for an equity line of credit using the new higher appraisal and your greatly expanded equity as collateral. Banks like home equity loans.

C) Borrow the down payment, settlement charges and any rehab costs by a home equity, hard money lender, credit cards, etc. After rehab, apply for FHA financing, which will order an appraisal. With the proceeds pay off the short-term financing. May give you enough for the down payment for your next purchase.

4. 30 Year, Fixed Rate, for Investors

In 2005-2006 all my financing was no-documentation 30 yr fixed, 80% LTV (Loan to Value). Sweet. You stated your income but didn't have to prove it. The press now calls it a "Liar loan". But it was a good vehicle for investors and small business people who used depreciation and rental expenses to cut down or eliminate taxes. The lender judged the loan by your credit score and balance sheet.

I like 30 yr (as opposed to 20 yr) mortgages because the payments are lower, thus increasing my Net **TODAY** and therefore also increasing my CASH ON CASH % **TODAY**!

The dollars I will pay from the 21st to the 30th year of a 30 year mortgage will be discounted heavily by inflation and the dropping value of the dollar. In the 21st year I project the dollar I pay will be worth 50% less than today and by the 30th year 75% less. So I want the monthly net money **TODAY** - higher Net and CASH ON CASH %. You may be different. Not a problem. Real estate accommodates all.

5. **No Money Down and Other Leverage Adventures**

No Money Down was the mantra of real estate gurus in the 1970s and continues to this day. Why? The guru market is a business unto itself. It has little to do with actually buying real estate. There are millions of people who can afford a book ($20), a real estate CD course ($500/$1,000) or a 3-day boot camp/conference/seminar ($1,995/$3,995) as opposed to the current 30/35% down payment for a rental house.

Hope springs eternal and the gurus sing a sweet song. Robert Allen (went bankrupt) had a best seller No Money Down then later No Money Down For the Nineties. Buy it used on Amazon.com. They are good reads and some concepts occasionally work. But if you finance 100% will you have a positive Net? Robert didn't.

THE PUSH UP BRA EFFECT OF DOWN PAYMENTS ON CASH ON CASH %

TOTAL HOUSE COST	DOWN PAYT	AMT FINAC	MTG RATE	PITI	RENT	GM	EXPENSES 17%	MO NET	Annual NET	CASH ON CASH%
$72,000	$2,500 3.5%	$69,500	FHA 6%	$738	$1,250	$512	$213	$299	$3,588	144%
$72,000	$14,500 20%	$57,500	FHA 6%	$652	$1,250	$598	$213	$385	$4,620	32%
$72,000	$21,500 30%	$50,500	FHA 6%	$602	$1,250	$648	$213	$435	$5,220	24%

The more you finance, the higher your Cash on Cash % is. However always be sure you have a positive cash flow.

Archimedes would like #1. I like #1. Cash On Cash over 100%. WOW!

Chapter Eighteen

Legal But Soooo Naughty Nice

The Magic of Interest, Depreciation, Taxes and Expenses

Mortgage interest and taxes paid, plus depreciation earned, plus business expenses (landlords run a business) may substantially reduce your taxable rental income or even bring it to zero. And, if you (1) manage the properties yourself (2) are not termed a professional investor according to your CPA and IRS guidelines, further rental losses may be deducted against your 1040 return, which includes W2 and other business or investment income. This may reduce or eliminate your entire Federal tax burden. The very rich have been riding these and other horses for eons with April 15th not a hurried nightmare, but a sweet and strangely satisfying triumph. It's actually quite simple. Stay with me.

1) **RENTAL NET INCOME FOR ONE HOUSE:** Rental Income minus PITI.

   a) $15,000 – **Annual Rental Income**

   b) $0 – **Principal paid is not a deduction.** The principal part of your mortgage payment reduces your mortgage balance but is not a deduction.

   c) ($5,500) – **Interest as a deduction.** You have a 20-year mortgage and pay $5,500 a year in interest. Interest is a deduction against your income. In January your bank, mortgage companies, credit cards, etc. will send you statements with the exact amount of interest you paid them in the past year. Give all of these to your CPA, as business related interest is deductible.

   d) ($3,000) – **Property Taxes is a deduction**

   e) ($600) - **Insurance is a deduction**

   f) $5900 – **Rental Net Income so far**

2) **DEPRECIATION MADE EASY:** I'll make this simple because it really is simple and even I understand it. DEPRECIATION EXAMPLE BELOW.

You buy a house for $80,000. Your CPA will define how much of the $80,000 is the cost of the land and how much is the cost of the house (or structure, as they call it). Your CPA determines the house is worth $64,000 (80%) and the land (the fixed or non-deductible part) $16,000 (20%).

The IRS allows you to depreciate the house over 30 years but not the land. The IRS assumes the house will be worthless in 30 years and therefore the annual deduction. It's a strange rule, since in the real world, the historical value of a house rises 3.5% a year, but I'm not going to argue.

$64,000 divided by 30 years = $2,133 depreciation or loss per year, for the next 30 years. Since you lost $2,133, your CPA will deduct that from your income and therefore you will not be taxed on it. Got it?

Depreciation 30 YRS: -2133 Deduction

3) COMPONENT DEPRECIATION: Your CPA will determine how the rehab and substantial maintenance work is to be depreciated by Component or with smaller maintenance work expensed outright.

You spent $30,000 on the rehab. There are different depreciation schedules (5 years—10 years—20 years—30 years) of Component Depreciation for different items and materials used. Your CPA will determine this. Let's say the $30,000 is Component Depreciated, on average (some 5 years, some 10 years, some 15 years), over 10 years. $30,000 divided by 10 years = $3,000 depreciation per year for the next ten years.

Component Depreciation: -3000 Deduction

4) MAINTENANCE REQUESTS/REPAIRS: Smaller repairs are generally expensed (100% deducted as a loss that year). Let's say you spent $2,000 on minor repairs performed by handymen and specialists and the CPA expenses it. That's $2,000 deducted from your income that year.

Maintenance Requests: -2000 Deduction

5) BUSINESS EXPENSES ARE SWEET: You now own a business with one or more rental properties. Folks who run businesses have expenses. Expenses may be deducted from your rental income and, if you qualify, other income, the sum of all your income we call gross income. Below is a list of normal business expenses you can deduct. I use QuickBooks during the year, every check goes in a category as it's written. I receive monthly income, expenses, and profit and loss reports. At the end of the year I download QuickBooks to my CPA and he determines all depreciation schedules, rental expenses, maintenance requests/repair expenses, and business expenses.

A) HOME BUSINESS: A portion of your home is used to run the business – a portion of heating, electricity, gas, taxes, insurance, repair, cable or FIOS, website, cell phone, home phone, etc. is deductible as a business expense.

B) TRAVEL EXPENSE: A portion, or entire amount, of a car's business use may be deducted. You can also write off car payments, gas, oil, tolls and insurance. An easy and simple way to write off auto is $0.50 per mile used for business. Train, bus, taxi, air or dog sled is also a deduction.

C) EDUCATION: Books, seminars, courses, conferences, real estate organizations, real estate vacations, real estate cruises, consultants, mentors. Education never stops.

D) ENTERTAINMENT: Lunch, dinner or entertainment (plays, concerts) with your real estate agent, lawyer, CPA, plumber, handyman etc. may be deducted. I write down what was discussed with who at the event on my monthly credit card statement.

E) CLOTHES: You may need certain types of clothes, shoes, jackets, suits, shirts, pants, socks, or ties for work.

F) FOOD: While working, you lunch or snack at McDonald's, Subway or a restaurant with your handyman. During the workday you need a bottle of water, Diet Coke, or morning coffee. Part of running your own business. Credit card is best.

G) OFFICE EQUIPMENT AND FURNITURE: Desks, cabinets, rugs, computers, fax, copier, lamps, wall decorations, window treatments.

H) OFFICE SUPPLIES: Paper, pens, erasers, printer ink, office supplies of all kinds. We buy online from Staples with a credit card.

I) OFFICE OR PARKING RENOVATION: Your home office or parking area may need to be reconfigured to fit your growing business. The rehab, painting, flooring, etc. costs will be determined as an expense-or to be depreciated by your CPA.

J) EMPLOYEES: I have a part-time bookkeeper, about 14 hours a week. Part-time assistant manager, about 20 hours a week. Part-time student gofer about 15 hours a week. I use QuickBooks Payroll. The independent contractors I use receive a 1099 form.

SUMMARY OF DEPRECIATION AND EXPENSES

A) Rental Income: +15000

    Interest: -5500 Deduction

    Taxes: -3000 Deduction

    Insurance: -600 Deduction

    Rental Net Income so far   5900

    Depreciation 30 yrs: -2133 Deduction

    Component Depreciation: -3000 Deduction

    Maintenance Expensed: -2000 Deduction

    Business Expenses: <u>-1750</u> Deduction

(2983) LOSS. Your CPA will determine if the loss may be deducted from your W2 income, other investments or other business income. Let's assume you can.

B) $40,000 Your W2 Income

    <u>- 2,983</u> Loss/Deduction from A

    $37,017 Adjusted income to be taxed

C)   If you have nine other (total 10) similar houses

    $37,017 Adjusted income from B

    <u>- 26,847</u> $2983 loss per house x 9 houses

    $10,170 Adjusted income to be taxed

D)   If you had one Tenant Turnover that year: Lost income $2,500

    Rehab $6500; Advertise $500; Total Loss $9500

    $10,170 Adjusted Income from C

    <u>-9,500</u> Tenant Turnover Loss

    $ 670 Income to pay tax on

How much Federal Tax did you pay last year? If you paid ZERO would you feel guilty or Soooo Naughty Nice?

AUDITS

In general the IRS is looking for bigger fish than you and me. One in approximately 500 returns are audited. If you keep reasonable records and follow the advice of your CPA, as I suggest you do in this chapter, you should be fine.

Be aware however, that the IRS is always looking for UNREPORTED INCOME. That's their hot button. Therefore all your rental income goes into the Rental Account be it checks, money orders or cash. All of it! A criminal tax attorney once told me, "The bulls make money. The bears make money. The pigs get slaughtered." Don't be a pig.

TEACHING POINT - Organization. There resides inside me an unorganized person always trying to get out and create chaos. I therefore try my darnedest to stay organized and follow my system. I pay everything by check or credit card so I have a trail. I rarely use cash. Different cards for different areas of my life. I fill shoeboxes (actually plastic bins) with my Home Depot, MAB, etc. receipts with house number and contractor's name on top. All checks written by hand or by a bookkeeper online, have a house street number on it and are assigned to that property when entered into Quickbooks.

TEACHING POINT – Credit Cards. When I receive my credit card statements, I immediately write, next to each charge, the house street number and a very brief explanation. Nothing fancy. 664 lunch CPA; 1309 MR Smith[15]; 427 Electric Abatelli; 1024 Plumbing Dennis. If no property is involved I explain; gas, lunch, office supplies, education etc. With 1309 MR Smith next to a Home Depot charge, my bookkeeper knows that MR means Maintenance Request, Smith is the Handyman, 1309 is the house to assign the repair cost to in QuickBooks. We track rehabs separately from repairs, since they are depreciated and the CPA may expense smaller repairs. 1450 Rehab next to a Home Depot charge would be entered under the 1450 Rehab in QuickBooks and therefore cumulative reports can be run. When I handwrite checks I put the house number (1024, 212 or 529) and a short note such as contractors name all on the left lower portion. The bookkeeper, online, views my handwritten checks when they are cashed, notes the

---

[15] MR means Maintenance Request, Smith is contractor's name

property number and category and assigns the charge in QuickBooks. The bookkeeper, who writes 80% of our checks online, does the same and assigns the charges in QuickBooks. I shoebox the actual receipts from Home Depot, MAB, gas, food, travel etc. and demand that the contractors write their name and the house number on the top of their Home Depot gift card receipts. Home Depot gift cards are how we have the contractors pay for material for jobs. We rarely use cash. In January, the bookkeeper downloads QuickBooks to the CPA and also sends all necessary paper including the banks, mortgage companies and credit card companies annual interest statements and any of that year's settlement sheets . The CPA puts it in order and I sign. It's a good system.

Chapter Nineteen

How to Become Very Rich Very Slowly

What do Evolution, Geography and Wealth Have In Common?

Spaceship Earth and its inhabitants, from the one-celled amoeba, to plants, to animals, to us, super important Homosapiens all evolved with small, sometimes infinitesimal, changes continually building upon previous changes over eons of time. This process is referred to by different names in each category or discipline, but the process appears to be the same.

GEOPHYSICAL SCIENCE EXPLAINS EARTH'S SLOW DEVELOPMENT

From a ball of hot gases to a cooling mass of matter to rock and earth and water. The large landmasses separated and moved .0005 of an inch per year and are now thousands of miles apart, mountains rise and disappear over eons, oceans wash land away only to create the new.

THE GROWTH OF LIFE ON EARTH IS CALLED EVOLUTION

From simple celled organisms to multi celled organisms to land based vertebra to Homosapiens. A glorious miracle of incremental changes over 5 billion years!

THE GROWTH OF WEALTH IS CALLED COMPOUNDING

The accumulation of wealth occurs over long periods of time. Slow and steady wins the race. Warren Buffet, speaking of wealth creating, makes the analogy of a young person (start young) being on top of a hill (higher the better) and guiding without much effort, a snowball down the hill, picking up bulk as it grows larger and larger over time (Warren's done about 22% per year over 50 years).

So it's compounding with small positive steps slowly building over time. May sound trite but it is one of the most powerful forces in the universe. Fortunes were and are being made, not overnight as promised by easy money hucksters, but over time – years, decades, 25 years, 50 years. Mistakes which lead to decreases are very costly. If you lose 50% of your wealth you must increase what is left by 100% just to break even. Ok, now let's bring compounding into our bricks and mortar business.

You have rehabbed a 3-bedroom to a 4 bedroom, with a one-car garage. Purchase price $50,000; settlement costs (2) $5,000; Rehab $29,000; Total $84,000. After rehab it is appraised for $120,000. Mortgage at 70% LTV or $84,000, thus zero cash invested or 100% financing. Your principal/interest payment is $690 mo, taxes $215, insurance $45, thus PITI is $950 mo.

Cash Invested	Rent	Garage		Total Rent	PITI	Gross Margin	Expenses	Mo. Net	Ann Net	100% Financing
$0	$1275/mo	+ $150	=	$1425	- $950	= $475/mo	- $200/mo	= $275	$3300	Yes

MAGIC TRICK #1—RENT HISTORICALLY INCREASES AT 2.5% ANNUALLY, but the mortgage principal and interest payments do not. As years pass this matters . . . a lot!

MAGIC TRICK #2—AFTER 20 YEARS THE MORTGAGE IS PAID OFF! (30 years if you were lucky/unlucky) Then the net income increases dramatically. Watch the figures JUMP! 20 years from today how old will you be? 45? 55? 65? It's gravy time.

MAGIC TRICK #3—HISTORICAL APPRECIATION OF HOUSE VALUE IS 3.5% ANNUALLY, COMPOUNDED! While the tenants pay the bills your house is appreciating (even while you sleep). Over 30 years compounding gets out of hand. Play Rip Van Winkle and wake up RICH! Caveat - from 2007 to 2012 we experienced a down cycle in appreciation. Yet the Fed continues to expand the money supply to pay their debts, fueling inflation, and history tells us that well located fixed assets (real estate) will, over the long term, continue its historical rise. (A bottle of Coke cost 10 cents 60 years ago!)

MAGIC TRICK #4—INTEREST, DEPRECIATION AND BUSINESS EXPENSES may eliminate or significantly reduce taxes paid on net income. It's a beautiful spring each April 15th with the Fed fertilizing your garden, not vice versa. Your CPA handles it.

MAGIC TRICK #5— RENT IN A NICHE. Have a wide moat protecting your net income and your ability to raise prices in the future. Your niches, because of where you live, may not be my niches but the vehicle doesn't matter, as long as it's a protected niche. If you live in or near a large older city you may enjoy the fruits of low supply and high demand of 4/5 bedroom houses, Section 8 Tenants, good school districts, garages, and student housing around a growing university. But you may find and exploit even better niches in your geographical area depending on the opportunities presented.

MAGIC TRICK #6—HOLD.   Don't sell regardless of circumstance, and all circumstances are temporary. Let compounding over time work for you. Bite the bullet. As you hold, you don't make a capital gains profit and therefore don't pay a capital gains tax. The tax that you didn't pay continues to compound. The difference is beyond huge. This is exactly what Warren Buffett does. Hold. If you need money, refinance because the proceeds are not taxable as they are not a capital gain.

MAGIC TRICK #7—YOU ARE NOT LIMITED TO ONE INVESTMENT HOUSE! You may buy as many as you are capable of finding, financing, and managing. Capitalism baby!

COMPOUNDING MAGIC!

Starting Point: House Value -- $120,000; Rent -- $1,275 mo;
Annual Net -- $3,300; Rents – 2.5% Annual Increase; All Expenses – 2.5% Annual Increase
House Value -- Historical Appreciation -- 3.5%

	1 house Net Income	House Value (3.5%)		5 houses Net Income	House Value (3.5%)		10 houses Net Income	House Value (3.5%)		20 houses Net Income	House Value (3.5%)
Year 1	$ 3,300	$ 120,000		$ 16,500	$ 600,000		$ 33,000	$1,200,000		$ 66,000	$2,400,000
Year 2	$ 3,590	$ 124,200		$ 17,948	$ 621,000		$ 35,895	$1,242,000		$ 71,790	$2,484,000
Year 3	$ 3,886	$ 128,547		$ 19,431	$ 642,735		$ 38,862	$1,285,470		$ 77,725	$2,570,940
Year 4	$ 4,190	$ 133,046		$ 20,952	$ 665,231		$ 41,904	$1,330,461		$ 83,808	$2,660,923
Year 5	$ 4,502	$ 137,703		$ 22,511	$ 688,514		$ 45,022	$1,377,028		$ 90,043	$2,754,055
Year 6	$ 4,822	$ 142,522		$ 24,109	$ 712,612		$ 48,217	$1,425,224		$ 96,434	$2,850,447
Year 7	$ 5,149	$ 147,511		$ 25,746	$ 737,553		$ 51,492	$1,475,106		$ 102,985	$2,950,213
Year 8	$ 5,485	$ 152,674		$ 27,425	$ 763,368		$ 54,850	$1,526,735		$ 109,700	$3,053,470
Year 9	$ 5,829	$ 158,017		$ 29,146	$ 790,085		$ 58,291	$1,580,171		$ 116,582	$3,160,342
Year 10	$ 6,182	$ 163,548		$ 30,909	$ 817,738		$ 61,818	$1,635,477		$ 123,637	$3,270,954
Year 11	$ 6,543	$ 169,272		$ 32,717	$ 846,359		$ 65,434	$1,692,719		$ 130,868	$3,385,437
Year 12	$ 6,914	$ 175,196		$ 34,570	$ 875,982		$ 69,140	$1,751,964		$ 138,279	$3,503,927
Year 13	$ 7,294	$ 181,328		$ 36,469	$ 906,641		$ 72,938	$1,813,282		$ 145,876	$3,626,565
Year 14	$ 7,683	$ 187,675		$ 38,416	$ 938,374		$ 76,832	$1,876,747		$ 153,663	$3,753,495
Year 15	$ 8,082	$ 194,243		$ 40,411	$ 971,217		$ 80,822	$1,942,433		$ 161,645	$3,884,867
Year 16	$ 8,491	$ 201,042		$ 42,456	$1,005,209		$ 84,913	$2,010,419		$ 169,826	$4,020,837
Year 17	$ 8,911	$ 208,078		$ 44,553	$1,040,392		$ 89,106	$2,080,783		$ 178,212	$4,161,566
Year 18	$ 9,340	$ 215,361		$ 46,702	$1,076,805		$ 93,403	$2,153,611		$ 186,807	$4,307,221
Year 19	$ 9,781	$ 222,899		$ 48,904	$1,114,494		$ 97,808	$2,228,987		$ 195,617	$4,457,974
Year 20	$ 10,232	$ 230,700		$ 51,162	$1,153,501		$ 102,324	$2,307,002		$ 204,647	$4,614,003

Hurray! Mortgage over! House Value now equals Owner's Equity. Expenses continue.

Year 21	$ 18,975	$ 238,775		$ 94,876	$1,193,873		$ 189,752	$2,387,747		$ 379,504	$4,775,493
Year 22	$ 19,450	$ 247,132		$ 97,248	$1,235,659		$ 194,496	$2,471,318		$ 388,991	$4,942,636
Year 23	$ 19,936	$ 255,781		$ 99,679	$1,278,907		$ 199,358	$2,557,814		$ 398,716	$5,115,628
Year 24	$ 20,434	$ 264,734		$ 102,171	$1,323,669		$ 204,342	$2,647,337		$ 408,684	$5,294,675
Year 25	$ 20,945	$ 273,999		$ 104,725	$1,369,997		$ 209,450	$2,739,994		$ 418,901	$5,479,988
Year 26	$ 21,469	$ 283,589		$ 107,343	$1,417,947		$ 214,687	$2,835,894		$ 429,373	$5,671,788
Year 27	$ 22,005	$ 293,515		$ 110,027	$1,467,575		$ 220,054	$2,935,150		$ 440,108	$5,870,301
Year 28	$ 22,556	$ 303,788		$ 112,778	$1,518,940		$ 225,555	$3,037,881		$ 451,110	$6,075,761
Year 29	$ 23,119	$ 314,421		$ 115,597	$1,572,103		$ 231,194	$3,144,206		$ 462,388	$6,288,413
Year 30	$ 23,697	$ 325,425		$ 118,487	$1,627,127		$ 236,974	$3,254,254		$ 473,948	$6,508,507
TOTALS	$ 23,697	$ 325,425		$ 118,487	$1,627,127		$ 236,974	$3,254,254		$ 473,948	$6,508,507

5 HOUSES	**30 YEARS**	**$118,487 ANNUAL NET**	**$1,627,127**	**OWNER'S EQUITY**
10 HOUSES	**30 YEARS**	**$236,974 ANNUAL NET**	**$3,254,254**	**OWNER'S EQUITY**
20 HOUSES	**30 YEARS**	**$473,948 ANNUAL NET**	**$6,508,507**	**OWNER'S EQUITY**

40 houses		75 houses		100 houses	
Net Income	House Value (3.5%)	Net Income	House Value (3.5%)	Net Income	House Value (3.5%)
$ 132,000	$ 4,800,000	$ 247,500	$ 9,000,000	$ 330,000	$12,000,000
$ 143,580	$ 4,968,000	$ 269,213	$ 9,315,000	$ 358,950	$12,420,000
$ 155,450	$ 5,141,880	$ 291,468	$ 9,641,025	$ 388,624	$12,854,700
$ 167,616	$ 5,321,846	$ 314,280	$ 9,978,461	$ 419,039	$13,304,615
$ 180,086	$ 5,508,110	$ 337,661	$ 10,327,707	$ 450,215	$13,770,276
$ 192,868	$ 5,700,894	$ 361,628	$ 10,689,177	$ 482,171	$14,252,236
$ 205,970	$ 5,900,426	$ 386,194	$ 11,063,298	$ 514,925	$14,751,064
$ 219,399	$ 6,106,940	$ 411,374	$ 11,450,513	$ 548,498	$15,267,351
$ 233,164	$ 6,320,683	$ 437,183	$ 11,851,281	$ 582,911	$15,801,708
$ 247,273	$ 6,541,907	$ 463,637	$ 12,266,076	$ 618,183	$16,354,768
$ 261,735	$ 6,770,874	$ 490,753	$ 12,695,389	$ 654,338	$16,927,185
$ 276,559	$ 7,007,855	$ 518,547	$ 13,139,727	$ 691,396	$17,519,637
$ 291,753	$ 7,253,130	$ 547,036	$ 13,599,618	$ 729,381	$18,132,824
$ 307,326	$ 7,506,989	$ 576,237	$ 14,075,605	$ 768,316	$18,767,473
$ 323,289	$ 7,769,734	$ 606,168	$ 14,568,251	$ 808,224	$19,424,334
$ 339,652	$ 8,041,674	$ 636,847	$ 15,078,139	$ 849,129	$20,104,186
$ 356,423	$ 8,323,133	$ 668,293	$ 15,605,874	$ 891,058	$20,807,832
$ 373,614	$ 8,614,443	$ 700,525	$ 16,152,080	$ 934,034	$21,536,107
$ 391,234	$ 8,915,948	$ 733,564	$ 16,717,403	$ 978,085	$22,289,870
$ 409,295	$ 9,228,006	$ 767,428	$ 17,302,512	$ 1,023,237	$23,070,016

Hurray! Mortgage over! House Value now equals Owner's Equity. Expenses continue.

40 houses		75 houses		100 houses	
$ 759,007	$ 9,550,987	$ 1,423,138	$ 17,908,100	$ 1,897,518	$23,877,466
$ 777,982	$ 9,885,271	$ 1,458,717	$ 18,534,883	$ 1,944,956	$24,713,178
$ 797,432	$10,231,256	$ 1,495,185	$ 19,183,604	$ 1,993,580	$25,578,139
$ 817,368	$10,589,350	$ 1,532,564	$ 19,855,030	$ 2,043,419	$26,473,374
$ 837,802	$10,959,977	$ 1,570,878	$ 20,549,956	$ 2,094,505	$27,399,942
$ 858,747	$11,343,576	$ 1,610,150	$ 21,269,205	$ 2,146,867	$28,358,940
$ 880,216	$11,740,601	$ 1,650,404	$ 22,013,627	$ 2,200,539	$29,351,503
$ 902,221	$12,151,522	$ 1,691,664	$ 22,784,104	$ 2,255,552	$30,378,805
$ 924,776	$12,576,825	$ 1,733,956	$ 23,581,548	$ 2,311,941	$31,442,063
$ 947,896	$13,017,014	$ 1,777,305	$ 24,406,902	$ 2,369,740	$32,542,536
$ 947,896	$13,017,014	$ 1,777,305	$ 24,406,902	$ 2,369,740	$32,542,536

40	HOUSES	30 YEARS	$ 947,896 ANNUAL NET	$13,017,014 OWNER'S EQUITY
75	HOUSES	30 YEARS	$1,777,305 ANNUAL NET	$24,406,902 OWNER'S EQUITY
100	HOUSES	30 YEARS	$2,369,740 ANNUAL NET	$32,542,536 OWNER'S EQUITY

I apologize that these numbers are so grotesquely outlandish. With 100 houses, after 30 years, an annual net income of $2,256,883 is obscene! Especially combined with owner's equity of $32,500,000. Compounding is like that. Let it work over time and it creates humongous numbers that ludicrously decimate your most optimistic "I am a millionaire" dreams.

In 1942 my Mom and Dad purchased a house on Long Island for $7000. Today, 69 years later, it's worth about $750,000. That's 107 times its' original price. After WWII Levittown Long Island sold manufactured ranch houses to returning WWII veterans for $90 down and $58 a month. In 1845 Henry David Thoreau built a 10x15 cabin on Walden Pond for $28.13. At that time an average wage for a day's work was $1. I could go on and on. Rest assured the federal government will inflate the money supply to pay its own debts and well-located income-producing real estate will rise in value.

In the last five years I've met real estate multi-millionaires, disguised as normal folks, who have done the aforementioned. Here are a few.

DISGUISED AS A HANDYMAN: Drives a pickup, work clothes, no college, does much of his own maintenance with 70 houses, mostly paid for. Likes vacations. Second house on the Chesapeake Bay with a 37' sailboat which he takes to the Caribbean once a year to stay at his 3rd house on St. Thomas.

DISGUISED AS A BANKER: Forty houses, all in one area, Media, the county seat. Investing for 30 years. Slow and steady. Buys low, rehabs, rents and holds. Because of the location of his houses, appreciation is well above 3.5%.

DISGUISED AS BLUE COLLAR HIGH SCHOOL BUDDIES: Philadelphia, 350 houses, which they sold on the top of the market in 2007, then started buying again. Work clothes, no college, rough tough. Personal houses at the New Jersey Shore. Race cars. Worth millions. Authors of Section 8 Bible and Section 8 Bible II. Recommended reading.

DISGUISED AS A REALTOR: Buying and holding for 50 years, over 400 houses, most or all paid for, wouldn't guess how astronomical his equity or net income is.

Surprisingly all of them direct their own tenant management with administrative and maintenance help. A few have unsuccessfully tried rental management companies.

All different personality types, different education levels, different talents, different niches but they did it. So can you. And me.

- The Millionaire Next Door. Thomas J. Stanley, Ph.D William D. Danko, Ph.D

Chapter Twenty

Full Disclosure

62 Reasons To Believe Me

Of the 70 real estate "How To" books on my shelf, the few excellent ones share one trait: credibility. I believed their stories. The authors weren't promoters hawking books with super wonderful money making concepts interspersed with RAH! RAH! motivation. The good books were real.

The best credibility flows directly from facts – the data backing up the claims. The following is a full disclosure spreadsheet of 12 columns containing figures of the houses we bought, rehabbed and rented, right down to the nearest dollar. This is the first "How to" real estate book I know of to offer full disclosure of properties purchased.

Below is an explanation of the columns:

1. Settlement date- the date we purchased the house.
2. Purchase price.
3. Number of bedrooms and baths after the rehab; not at time of purchase.
4. Does it have a garage?
5. Current market value - my best educated guess as a rented investment property.
6. Current equity - #5, current market value, minus the mortgage balance.
7. Monthly rent.
8. PITI - Principle, Interest, Taxes and Insurance.
9. Gross margin - Rent minus PITI.
10. Expense = Administration + Maintenance + Vacancy. Averages 17% of monthly house rents and $8 per month per garage.
11. Monthly Net - Rent minus PITI minus Expenses.
12. Annual Net - Monthly Net x 12 months.

62 Houses, 21 Garages, 3 Million Equity, 22,000 Net a Month, in 7 Yrs.

ID	Settled	Purchase Price	After Rehab Bed/ Bath	Garage	Current Market Value	Current Equity **	Mo. Rent	Prin. Int Taxes Ins (PITI)	Gross Margin	Monthly Expenses ***	Monthly Net	Annual Net
1	2/4/05	$25,000	3BR-1B	-	$94,000	$54,550	$1,080	471	$609	$184	$425	**$5,105**
2	2/9/05	43,500	4BR-1.5B	-	110,000	49,750	1,230	599	$631	$209	$422	**$5,063**
3	3/2/05	117,900	4BR-1B	1	199,000	79,580	1,516	1,140	$376	$238	$138	**$1,656**
4	3/4/05	100,000	4BR-1.5B	-	202,000	96,763	1,420	1,111	$309	$241	$68	**$811**
5	3/18/05	43,500	3BR-1B	-	94,000	53,145	1050	487	$563	$179	$385	**$4,614**
6	4/8/05	64,500	4BR-1B	-	110,000	52,026	1,235	608	$627	$210	$417	**$5,005**
7	4/8/05	52,000	4BR-1B	-	80,000	25,877	1260	574	$686	$214	$472	**$5,662**
8	5/6/05	58,000	4BR-1B	-	135,000	77,122	1,320	652	$668	$224	$444	**$5,323**
9	5/9/05	68,100	4BR-1.5B	-	110,000	41,425	1,199	665	$534	$204	$330	**$3,962**
10	5/23/05	79,000	3BR-1B	-	133,000	71,505	1,125	678	$447	$191	$256	**$3,069**
11	6/28/05	45,500	4BR-1B	-	135,000	64,264	1,460	798	$662	$248	$414	**$4,966**
12	7/11/05	62,000	4BR-1B	-	110,000	44,710	1,233	671	$562	$210	$352	**$4,229**
13	7/25/05	58,000	4BR-1B	-	110,000	40,791	1,289	456	$833	$219	$614	**$7,366**
14	8/31/05	105,000	4BR-2B	-	140,000	50,230	1,313	981	$332	$223	$109	**$1,305**
15	12/12/05	41,000	5BR-1.5B	-	160,000	56,666	1,332	955	$377	$226	$151	**$1,807**
16	1/12/06	79,900	4BR-1B		194,400	49,754	1,400	1,361	$39	$238	($199)	**($2,388)**
17	2/5/06	49,900	4BR-1.5B	-	140,000	46,473	1,300	961	$339	$221	$118	**$1,416**
18	3/27/06	104,900	5BR-1.5B	4	225,000	107,308	2,568	1,222	$1,346	$281	$1,065	**$12,780**
19	5/12/06	65,000	5BR-1.5B	2	180,000	52,854	2,150	1,294	$856	$280	$576	**$6,912**
20	5/26/06	65,500	4BR-2B	1	135,000	41,763	1,450	837	$613	$227	$386	**$4,632**
21	5/30/06	56,100	4BR-1B	-	110,000	21,450	1,245	808	$437	$212	$225	**$2,704**
22	7/20/06	80,000	5Br-2B	-	125,000	35,700	1,450	876	$574	$247	$328	**$3,930**
23	7/28/06	61,000	4BR-1.5B	-	125,000	37,936	1,230	750	$480	$209	$271	**$3,251**

ID	Settled	Purchase Price	After Rehab Bed/ Bath	Garage	Current Market Value	Current Equity **	Mo. Rent	Prin. Int Taxes Ins (PITI)	Gross Margin	Monthly Expenses ***	Monthly Net	Annual Net
24	8/28/06	25,000	5BR-1.5B	-	150,000	44,563	1,435	984	$451	$244	$207	$2,485
25	8/28/06	77,500	3BR-1B	-	137,000	58,500	1,066	784	$282	$181	$101	$1,209
26	12/13/06	56,500	5BR-1.5B	-	145,000	50,152	1,500	890	$610	$255	$355	$4,260
27	1/27/07	27,000	3BR-1B	1	100,000	65,000	1,228	505	$723	$194	$529	$6,348
28	10/31/07	51,500	4BR-2B	1	130,000	42,785	1,710	1,025	$685	$255	$430	$5,160
29	12/31/07	65,000	5BR-2B	6	260,000	141,955	2,000	1,367	$633	$256	$377	$4,524
30	5/22/08	*44,000	5BR-1B	1	145,000	56,001	1,600	987	$613	$255	$358	$4,296
31	11/21/08	*70,000	5BR-1.5B	-	145,000	76,864	1,460	950	$510	$248	$262	$3,142
32	11/24/08	*64,000	4BR-1B	-	135,000	76,585	1,302	675	$627	$221	$406	$4,868
33	3/9/09	*52,000	5BR-1.5B	-	130,000	50,490	1,425	785	$640	$242	$398	$4,773
34	4/1/09	73,020	4BR-1B	-	125,000	56,044	1,275	716	$559	$217	$342	$4,107
35	4/9/09	*75,100	4BR-2B	1	145,000	48,070	1,450	1,045	$405	$247	$159	$1,902
36	6/10/09	60,100	4BR-1B	-	110,000	40,285	1,307	775	$532	$222	$310	$3,718
37	7/15/09	52,000	5BR-1B	-	140,000	75,000	1,300	764	$536	$221	$315	$3,780
38	7/15/09	52,000	4BR-1B	-	110,000	49,560	1,307	719	$588	$222	$366	$4,390
39	12/3/09	47,500	6BR-2B(S)	-	220,000	89,800	1,900	1,378	$522	$323	$199	$2,388
40	2/1/10	50,000	4BR 1.5B	-	120,000	41,800	1,325	900	$425	$225	$200	$2,397
41	2/23/10	50,000	4BR/1B	-	110,000	46,100	1,307	712	$595	$222	$373	$4,474
42	3/5/10	44,100	4BR-1.5B	-	110,000	47,800	1,230	739	$491	$209	$282	$3,383
43	3/31/10	*124,000	6BR-2B(S)	-	240,000	52,000	1,900	1,321	$579	$323	$256	$3,072
44	4/19/10	40,000	6BR 2B	-	120,000	51,255	1,675	810	$865	$285	$580	$6,963
45	5/15/10	19,000	5BR-1.5B	-	145,000	72,270	1,500	769	$731	$255	$476	$5,712
46	5/26/10	42,500	4BR-1B	-	130,000	61,269	1,300	769	$531	$221	$310	$3,720
47	8/18/10	*107,900	6BR-2B(S)	1	220,000	50,000	2,200	1,200	$1,000	$374	$626	$7,512
48	9/10/10	35,000	4BR-1.5B	-	125,000	49,615	1,375	811	$564	$234	$330	$3,963

ID	Settled	Purchase Price	After Rehab Bed/ Bath	Garage	Current Market Value	Current Equity **	Mo. Rent	Prin. Int Taxes Ins (PITI)	Gross Margin	Monthly Expenses ***	Monthly Net	Annual Net
49	1/31/11	45,000	5BR-1.5B	1	135,000	51,800	1,525	919	$606	$259	$347	**$4,161**
50	2/24/11	45,000	5BR-2B	1	120,000	43,650	1,450	913	$537	$247	$291	**$3,486**
51	3/14/11	35,000	4BR-1.5B	-	110,000	54,750	1,300	633	$667	$221	$446	**$5,352**
52	4/22/11	42,000	4BR-1.5B	-	110,000	49,625	1,300	627	$673	$221	$452	**$5,424**
53	5/13/11	23,400	5BR-1.5B	-	110,000	50,055	1,450	656	$794	$247	$548	**$6,570**
54	5/13/11	23,400	4BR-1.5B	-	110,000	67,300	1,300	473	$827	$221	$606	**$7,272**
55	5/13/11	23,400	4BR-1.5B	-	110,000	75,148	1,300	453	$847	$221	$626	**$7,512**
56	5/13/11	23,400	4BR-1.5B	-	110,000	77,240	1,300	383	$917	$221	$696	**$8,352**
57	5/13/11	23,400	4BR-1.5B	-	110,000	75,856	1,300	386	$914	$221	$693	**$8,316**
58	6/10/11	26,000	4BR-1.5B	-	135,000	72,287	1,300	558	$742	$221	$521	**$6,252**
59	9/21/11	40,000	5BR-1.5B	-	110,000	22,500	1,500	985	$515	$255	$260	**$3,120**
60	10/13/11	40,000	4BR-1.5B	-	110,000	30,000	1,350	906	$444	$230	$215	**$2,574**
61	12/21/11	38,200	5BR-2B	-	125,000	37,500	1,450	950	$500	$247	$254	**$3,042**
62	12/30/11	25,000	4BR-1.5B	-	110,000	68,000	1,300	526	$774	$221	$553	**$6,636**
TOTAL		$2,846,220		21	$8,418,400	$3,521,116	$88,057	$50,703	$37,354	$14,538	$22,816	$273,793
	* Kid's Houses (7)											
	S = Student Rentals (3)											
	** Current Equity = Market Value minus Mortgage Balance											
	*** Monthly Administration, Maintenance, Vacancy = Expenses which equals 17% of Monthly Rent											

Author's Confession: When I started in 2005, my sole objective was to create a monthly income. Building equity was not in the equation. During the last seven years, I rarely gave a passing thought to the increasing equity. I was shocked when I saw the current equity total, but compounding is like that, it has its own engine. You just turn the key and hang on.

"It was never my thinking that made big money. It was always my sitting. Men who can both be right and sit tight are uncommon." – Jesse Lauriston Livermore

Chapter Twenty One

Forms, Leases, Contracts, Specification of Material and Methods

Purchase at http://www.delcohomerental.com and receive a free newsletter

Excel Spreadsheets/Data Sheets- to keep the business organized

1. **Mortgage spreadsheets**

   Property address, mortgage company, account number, interest/terms/loan-to-value, principal, interest, tax and insurance (PITI), etc.

2. **Insurance policies data sheet**

   Property, insurance company, policy number, insured amount, premium, etc.

3. **Tenant spreadsheet**

   Property, tenant name, phone numbers (such as home, cell, work), rent, etc.

4. **Tenant birthdays and rental anniversary dates**

   By month, the birthdays and anniversaries by tenant date. We send out cards seven days before event date and include a Wal-Mart gift certificate for anniversary dates.

5. **Rental Payments spreadsheet**

   We use Excel and include the property, tenant name, security deposit, date of security deposit, rent, date the rent started, column for each month of calendar year (starting with January) - next to each month we have "Late" - as rent comes in we put in rent amount and date on envelope (VERY IMPORTANT because date on envelope is date paid). This spreadsheet is used all the time - every day.

6. **Anniversary Rental Renewal dates**

   By month (starting with January), we have property address, the original date and rent of lease.

   Example: 2007 rent, date the adjustment was sent, date it was put in effect

   2008 rent, date the adjustment was sent, date it was put in effect

7. Monthly Principal Paid

Positive reminder to ourselves of APPROXIMATELY how much we are paying off per month. Redone on annual basis in January.

8. District Court Notices

We have all District Court forms ready to use in bins and we do use them.

9. Big Spreadsheet (all dates, financial, rental, etc. on each house)

The "mother" of all spreadsheets - It has all the financial information we like to look at:

- Number of properties
- Property address
- Purchase price
- Date of settlement
- Closing costs
- Improvements/Rehab
- Interest paid on financing for rehab
- Refinance costs- settlement costs
- Total costs
- Appraised value
- Refi- Terms (such as interest, term, LTV)
- Mortgage amount
- Cash invested
- Current value
- Equity
- Principal Interest Taxes Insurance (PITI)
- Rent/Month
- Gross margin
- Expenses (17%)
- Net for month
- Annual net

10. Property data sheet (physical data on each house)

Entails all physical characteristics of property, from lot size to what type of dryer you have (gas/electric), garage size, etc

11. Monthly Cash Profit and Loss (monthly and year-to-date)

By the tenth of the following month, we know on cash basis where we are. No depreciation or principal paid in, etc. Very helpful.

House Purchase Forms

1. Pre-offer Property Worksheet

To be filled out BEFORE the 1st offer. Makes you look at the numbers before committing.

2. New Purchased Property checklist

Invaluable, allows you to list everything that needs to be done up until settlement.

3. Agreement of Sale (two-page)

Simple yet legally correct agreement of sale. Used with individual sellers.

4. Lien Search

One page, fax it to search company, they will uncover liens on a property. Used before a sheriff sale to ascertain the liens besides the one that is forcing the sheriff sale.

Contractor Agreement and Forms

1. Contractor Application

I wish I had this when I started out - it would have saved me a lot of money and heartache. Essentially an application, one page, but has all pertinent information plus background plus referrals with phone numbers.

2. Contractor Agreement

The Gold Standard in contractor agreements. Seven parts, use all seven. Get ready for battle.

3. Independent Contractor Services Agreement

Actual agreement, 3 pages, comprehensive

Exhibit A – Scope of Work: Lines out in great detail the scope of the work. For an entire house rehab, it doesn't let you miss a thing.

Exhibit B – Specifications of Methods and Materials: This 30-page document is a small, very specific "How To" book on rehabbing a rental house. Includes 45 items of "ELIMINATORS"—things not to have in a rental house. For anyone who wants to rehab a rental house, this section is invaluable. Worth $2500 alone. Includes Home Depot's SKU and price of all materials to be used in rehab. A Rehab Bible. Includes everything! Just look it up!

Exhibit C – Payment Schedule: Pay as work is being accomplished. Do not alter this schedule because they cry a lot, moan, tell colorful stories of impending calamity, etc.

Exhibit D – Change Order Form: If there are changes, put it in writing, signed by both parties

Exhibit E – Punch List: Most used part of agreement. Go in each Friday with the punch list with carbon and second page. Walk around, make a list. Leave original with the contractor.

Exhibit F – Responsibility for Damage: Just to make sure any damage they cause is their responsibility

4. Contract Tracking

Mailed to contractor's home by Monday after a Friday draw is given to them. Lines out where they are in contract concerning money and time left to complete the work. All contracts have an end date after which they are charged $100 a day.

5. Contractor Agreement for Use of Gift Cards

We use Home Depot gift cards to find some contractor's purchase of material. Be very careful.

6. Hourly Time Sheets

If you have hourly workers, this is the sheet to use. But we also have them call in when starting at a property, call out when leaving. Administration has a computer sign in/out payroll program.

7. Materials Sign Out

If you give a contractor anything from your warehouse, have them sign them out.

8. Equipment on Loan

If you have machines or tools and you loan them out, get them to sign an Equipment on Loan form or you will never see them again.

Prospective Tenants

1. Rental Application

4 pages, the foundation of the tenant choice system. When the tenant is finished, go over every item with them, ask for information not completed. After the process you know a great deal and you then rate the tenant 1 to 3. A beautiful, thorough start to a very important process.

2. Prospective Tenant Checklist

A checklist to guide and remind you through the tenant choice process. Don't skip a step! It may cost you $10,000 or more! That's not a joke.

3. Home Visit Checklist

Yes, we visit their current residence! One page form filled out after the current home visit. Guides you to record everything. Then you again rate the prospect 1-3.

4. Landlord Verification

Contact the former and current landlord before making a decision.

Lease Forms

1. Lease

Seven parts, 26 pages, covers everything conceivable, and some inconceivable but happens anyway, and therefore protects you as the landlord. Tenant initials every page, signs last page. Part 7 - Highlights of Lease is a compilation of the most important paragraphs of lease, which is read aloud to tenant and they initial each of the 30 highlights.

Part 1 – Residential Lease – 13 pages, 55 paragraphs, a work of art.

Part 2 – Lead Paint – 1 page plus a federal pamphlet to hand out.

Part 3 – Utility TURN ON – 2 pages. Guides them to putting utilities and cable in their name. Includes phone numbers, etc.

Part 4 – Tenant Move-In/Landlord Move-Out – Five-page inventory checklist ending with a one-page price list for broken or missing items. Very helpful when tenant moves out leaving a mess but still wants their security deposit back!

Part 5 – Maintenance Request Letter – They initial they received 2 Maintenance Requests, agree to use them, etc. Includes Part 5a, Maintenance Request form.

Part 6 – Rental Deposit – 1 page. How much is their security deposit? How much have they currently paid? A schedule of future security deposit payments with dates to be postmarked by, then 12 paragraphs outlining how a tenant gets their security deposit back, which is a copy of paragraph 23 in the lease. Brilliant!

Part 7 – Highlights of Lease – 2 pages, 30 2 or 3-line paragraphs describing the most frequently violated issues, each of which the tenant initials. If then violated, we highlight the violated paragraph and their initials and mail a copy to them.

2. Garage Lease

One page, simple, to the point. After 15 days of non-payment, you can change locks and sell their goods. A commercial lease has no protection from the landlord-tenant law.

3. Pet Agreement

We don't allow pets! But if we make an exception it costs the tenant money per month and an extra security deposit. One page, simple, to the point. If the pet does not work out, you can get rid of it.

Tenant Management

1. Tenant Turnover Administrative Checklist

Organizes the process for the administrative manager, includes all steps required for the next tenant.

2. Notice of Lease Violation

Used to notify tenants of specific violations observed or reported. Always include a copy of Lease Highlights with the violation and tenant's initials highlighted.

3. Notice to Pay or Move

Final notice before legal action. Usually gets results.

4. Notice of Late Charges

Identifying tenant's late charges now owed.

5. Notice of Insufficient Funds

Identifying incident and associated fees due.

6. Memo

Informal letterhead sheet by which you can communicate with a tenant.

7. Notice to Vacating Tenant

Once we receive or give notice to vacate, we send this form 3 times. Has 9 things they must do to receive their security deposit back. Very effective.

8. Notice of Rent Increase

9. Notice of Lease Termination

10. Agreement for Tenant Alteration

We don't allow alterations. But we have a process for denial. If tenant requests permission to alter property, they fill out a Tenant Alteration form by which they agree to put property back to condition as it was when they moved in.

11. Notice of Open House Dates

When tenant gives notice to move, we schedule open house for prospective tenants.

12. Notice of Maintenance Appointment

Mailed to tenant, with day of week and date, always with a 3 or 4-hour window of starting.

13. Maintenance Request Form

Mailed by tenants outlining things in need of repair. Landlord uses internally and forwards to handyman or contractor.

14. Notice of Upcoming Inspection Form

Mailed to alert tenant of municipal or housing inspections.

15. Inspection Checklist

Used by handymen and contractors to identify areas of concern while at the property. To be used before an upcoming inspection.

16. Tenant Turnover Rehab Checklist

Helps the landlord identify all areas to be addressed by the contractor before the next tenant moves in.

General Administration Forms

17. Application for Employment

Two pages, to the point, goes by legal guidelines

18. Drug Test and where to obtain such

If you believe a tenant or a contractor is using drugs, ask them to take a drug test where the methodology is to use hair (The Gold Standard).

19. To-Do List

Old standard used everyday - perhaps so should you.

Bibliography

Allen, R. G. (2004). *Nothing Down for the 2000s.* New York: Free Press.

Beck, D. (2004). *Down to Earth Landlording.* Beach Grove: Skyward Publising.

Blanchard, K. (1991). *The One Minute Manager.* Minneapolis: Quill.

Butler, M. (2006). *Landlording on Autopilot.* Hoboken: Wiley.

Carnegie, D. (1997). *How to Win Friends and Influence People.* New York: Simon & Schuster Adult Publishing.

Cipriano, N., & McLean, M. (2006). *The Section 8 Bible.* Nick Cipriano & Michael Mclean.

Cohen, H. (1982). *You Can Negotiate Anything.* New York: Bantam.

Collins, J. (2001). *Good to Great.* New York: The Principal Followed by Great Companies.

Collins, J., & Porras, J. (2002). *Built to Last: Successful Habits of Visionary Companies.* New York: Harper Business.

Crosby, P. (1980). *Quality is Free.* Mentor Publishing.

Cunningham, L. (2008). *The Essays of Warren Buffet. Lessons for Corporate America.* Cunningham Group.

Danko, W. D., & Stanley, T. J. (1996). *The Millionaire Next Door.* New York: Pocket Books.

Drucker, P. (1993). *The Effective Executive.* New York: Harper Business.

Drucker, P. (2008). *The Five Most Important Questions You Will Ever Ask About Your Organization.* San Francisco: Jossey- Bass.

Eldred, G. W. (2009). *Investing in Real Estate.* Hoboken: John Wiley & Sons.

Fisher, R., & Ury, W. (1986). *Getting to Yes.* New York: Random House Adult Publishing.

Fox, D. (2004). *From Credit Repair to Credit Millionaires.* By Special Arrangments Publishing.

Gallinelli, F. (2009). *What Every Real Estate Investor Needs to Know About Cash Flow... and 36 Other Key Financial Measures.* New York: McGraw-Hill Company.

Geyen, M. (2004). *University Wealth: 21 Secrets to Buy & Manage Student Rental Property.* Columbus: Ascend Beyond Publishing.

Jay, A. (1996). *Management and Machiavelli.* Upper Saddle River: Prentice Hall Press.

Karrass, C. (1986). *Give and Take.* New York: Random House Adult Trade Publishing Group.

Machiavelli, N. (1984). *The Prince.* New York: Bantam Classics.

Nickerson, W. (1959). *How I turned $1,000 into a Million in Real Estate- In My Spare Time.* New York: Simon and Schuster.

Peters, T., & Waterman, R. (1985). *In Search of Excellence.* Audio Partners Publishing Corporation.

Roger, J., & McWilliams, P. (1992). *Do it! Lets Get Off Our Buts.* Los Angeles: Prelude Press.

Schaub, J. (2005). *Building Wealth One House at a Time.* New York: McGraw Hill Companies.

Schroeder, A. (2008). *The Snowball: Warren Buffet and the Business of Life.* New York: Bantam Dell.

Schumacher, D. (2004). *Buy and Hold.* New York: Schumacher Enterprises.

Schumacher, D. T. (1992). *The Buy and Hold Real Estate Strategy : How to Secure Profits in Any Real Estate Market.* New York: Wiley.

Taylor, J. (2002). *The Landlord's Kit.* New York: Kaplan Publishing.

Zaransky, M. H. (2006). *Profit by Investing in Student Housing.* New York: Kaplan Publisihing.

Made in the USA
Lexington, KY
25 November 2012